Not My Responsibility

Setting Healthy Boundaries, Ending Co-Dependency, & Managing Toxic Relationships

Blythe Bailey

SWH Media

Copyright © 2023 by Blythe Bailey

SWH Media, LLC

All rights reserved.

No portion of this book may be reproduced in any form without written permission from the publisher or author, except as permitted by U.S. copyright law.

CONTENTS

Foreword	V
1. Are You Taking Reponsibility for Things You Shouldn't?	1
2. A Meditation for Letting Go of Things That Aren't My Responsibility	7
3. Accepting Limitations of Responsibility	13
4. A Meditation: I Am Not Responsible for Fixing Everything for Everyone	19
5. But I Have To.....	21
6. A Meditation: It is not my responsibility to rescue everyone	27
7. Setting Healthy Boundaries and the Power of No	33
8. A Meditation on Setting Boundaries	41
9. Why do we do this?	45
10. A Meditation on Overcoming Codependence	53
11. Recognizing Narcissists and Other Toxic People	57

12.	A Meditation for Healing From a Relationship With a Narcissist	65
13.	Toxic Relationships	69
14.	A Meditation for Healing From a Toxic Relationship	73
15.	Narcissitic Parents and Boundaries	77
16.	A Meditation for Healing From a Narcissistic Parent	83
17.	Boundary Setting with Toxic People	91
18.	A Meditation to Stop Enabling Others Behaviors	97
19.	Boundary Setting at Work	101
20.	The Power of Saying No: A Meditation	105
21.	Living Your Life in a Supporting Role	109
22.	A Meditation: I Can Be the Star of My Own Life	113
23.	Dealing with Guilt	119
24.	A Meditation on Eliminating Feelings of Guilt	125
25.	The Importance of Self Care	129
26.	A Meditation on Protecting my Peace	133
27.	Yoga to Release Stresss and Trauma in Our Bodies	137
28.	Deep Breathing Exercises	149
29.	EFT, Emotional Freedom Technique	153
30.	Resources	161

FOREWORD

Growing up as an only child, I always felt that I was different from other children. My parents treated me like a miniature adult rather than a typical child. I was told over and over that I was mature for my age.

At the time, I felt proud of these compliments. I felt special, like I was ahead of my peers in terms of my emotional and intellectual development. As I grew older and had children of my own, I realized that this was not a normal way for a child to be treated.

I realized that my childhood was not as idyllic as I had once thought.

I realized that my parent's expectations of me were not just high; they were unrealistic. They expected me to be perfect. When I made mistakes, my parents made me feel like a failure instead of a learning child.

Children need the freedom to play, explore and make mistakes. When they are constantly told that they are mature or shamed for making mistakes, it can lead to them feeling like they are not allowed to make mistakes or have fun like other children. This can create a sense of isolation and loneliness, which can affect their social and emotional development.

Being treated like an adult at a young age can lead to premature independence. When children are treated like adults, they may feel that they are expected to be self-sufficient and not rely on others for help. This can lead to them feeling like they have to figure everything out on their own, which can be overwhelming and damaging to their mental health.

This type of parenting can be incredibly damaging to a child's self-esteem and emotional well-being. When a child is constantly told that they are mature for their age, they may feel like they are not allowed to be a child. They may feel like they have to take on adult responsibilities and act in a certain way in order to gain approval from their parents. It can lead to feelings of pressure, anxiety, and a lack of freedom to be a child.

This can have long-lasting effects on a person's mental health and self-esteem.

Children are not meant to carry the weight of adult responsibilities.

From a young age, I have always felt a strong sense of responsibility and have taken it upon myself to look out for the well-being of those around me. This became an integral part of my character, motivating me to prioritize the needs of others over my own. My father told me that I was strong like he was and that it was our job to take care of my mother, protect her and navigate parts of the world that were difficult for her.

As I got older, my sense of duty only intensified, and I became the go-to person for friends, family, and my spouse.

Being needed became synonymous with being loved.

In my quest to be the dependable one, I neglected my own desires and aspirations. I developed chronic pain and health issues from the intense pressure of feeling responsible for things that weren't my burden to bear.

I spent the thirteen years I was married to my first husband, making sure he had the support he needed to reach his goals and achieve his dreams. We built a wildly successful life by anyone's standards, building a seven-figure business together.

I did 'life' for him. Paid the bills, cleaned the house, did all the cooking, booked his plane tickets, packed his suitcases, ran our seven-figure business with him, and raised our children.

I buried my dreams. I buried my ambition, and my desires in the service of his.

There was no gratitude from him for the things I did for him. He expected it.

As time went on, I resented him and the fact that he took so much from me without giving anything back. He expected me to put him first. To take on his responsibilities and make them my own.

When we had our first child, our marriage floundered.

Our firstborn son was a high-needs baby, and I was exhausted from caring for him. I had very little energy left for my needy and demanding husband.

My husband resented that he was no longer the center of my world. Even though I still did his laundry, cooked his meals, and helped him with his business, I was busy mothering and didn't have the time or energy for him that he demanded.

When I was pregnant with our second child, I had terrible

morning sickness that lasted for five months. I could hardly care for myself and our three-year-old. I couldn't give him the attention he demanded.

One evening, he called me to tell me he was on his way home. I asked him to get dinner because I wasn't feeling well.

He got food for himself.

Nothing for me.

Nothing for our three-year-old.

He didn't understand my anger that he didn't even think of us. He said I was overreacting.

Two months after our second planned baby was born, I found out he was having an affair with his secretary.

He'd been cheating for months.

Taking her on 'work trips' while I was pregnant.

When I confronted him, he swore up and down that he wasn't cheating. Then he cleaned out our savings, changed the locks on our house when I was at my parents with our four-year-old and newborn, and canceled our health insurance and my cell phone.

The story gets worse but is not in the scope of this book.

I gave everything I had to him for thirteen years and it wasn't enough.

Because it is never enough when you are dealing with a toxic person.

I spent years after our divorce feeling guilty for putting myself and my children in this position.

For every terrible thing that my ex did to my kids, I blamed myself.

It didn't help that my mother told me that I had brought this on our family and on my children.

Over the years, I remarried. My husband has an autoimmune disease and almost died after a botched surgery when we'd only been married a year.

I made it my mission to heal him. I dove into research on healing foods, medical treatments, and alternative therapies.

He would tell our friends and family that he would be dead if it weren't for me.

Every time he would have a setback, it would fill me with terror that I would fail him and not be able to help him feel better. That he might die if I didn't figure out what to do to help him.

When my husband's health prevented him from doing the physical job he had been doing previously, I helped him buy a business and helped him run it, all while caring for my youngest son had serious health issues that required my constant care. I took care of all of the household chores, all of the parenting and caregiving…after all, they were my kids, not his biological ones so I felt that I couldn't put any responsibility for their care on him.

My husband never volunteered to help with anything. Having serious health issues since the age of thirteen had gotten my husband used to everyone treating him with kid gloves, and babying him.

I was used to taking care of my ex-husband and my mother. I told myself that my husband was sick, so he really needed me to do everything. That he wasn't being selfish, he was just not able to handle more.

My own health failed as I cared for my husband and my children, helped with his business, and fought off multiple custody battles filed by my ex-husband.

I was burnt out, anxious, depressed, and in terrible pain.

I went to my long-term doctor and explained to him I could barely walk. That my legs felt so heavy, I could hardly climb the stairs in our home.

He had been our family doctor for the better part of a decade. He'd supported my family through my husband's illness, cared for my youngest son who had multiple health problems, and treated our family through many crises.

He looked into my eyes and said, "Blythe, of course, you can hardly walk. You are carrying the weight of the world on your shoulders. You need to let go of the things that aren't your responsibility."

He told me that I wasn't responsible for my ex-husband's behavior toward our children.

He said I wasn't responsible for keeping my husband alive.

He told me that I wasn't responsible for the state of the world.

It was a life-changing conversation.

I had spent decades feeling as if the entire world would fall apart and my family would be hurt, or maybe even die, if I didn't do everything for everyone.

I didn't know what to do with this information.

How could I just let go of the weight of responsibility that was crushing me, weighing me down?

How could I let go of the responsibilities when my family

needed me?

My worry was the only thing keeping the world turning.

Things came to a head when I got very sick a few months later. I wasn't sick for a day or two but for weeks.

Our normal family dynamic of me being the caregiver was knocked on its head. It didn't go well.

I had been doing all the day-to-day chores that kept our family functioning and when I couldn't do it, my husband didn't pick up the slack. He resented having to do things like feed our family when I couldn't.

It took me back to being pregnant with my youngest child and my ex-husband getting food for himself and not for our firstborn or me. I felt unloved and resentful.

The patterns of the past had repeated themselves and I knew it needed to end. That I couldn't…. wouldn't…. live the rest of my life taking on all the responsibility for everyone in my life when they wouldn't take care of me when I needed it.

Over the course of the next few months, I did a lot of work on myself. I realized that I had been replicating the same patterns of making myself small in service of my husband, my children, and my parents, that I had made during my first marriage, and that I had learned during my dysfunctional childhood.

I was approaching fifty years old and had accomplished nothing that I wanted in my life because I had spent my entire adult life putting my needs, wants, and desires aside for everyone in my life.

That was the beginning of a lot of conversations and some therapy.

Epiphanies were made.

The most eye-opening to me was the day my husband of over a decade said, "But you are a caregiver by nature. You like taking care of people."

I was shocked at his statement. It felt like he didn't even know me.

I am not a caregiver by nature. I do not 'like' taking care of people.

Instead, I am hyper-responsible, have a deep sense of duty, and do the things that need to be done, even at great sacrifice to myself.

That hyper-responsibility and sense of duty were weighing on me so heavily that my health was wrecked.

I was being weighed down by all the responsibility I had taken on that wasn't mine to bear.

Something needed to change.

I needed to change if I was going to survive.

After eleven years of marriage, there was a huge renegotiation of our relationship.

Thankfully, my husband was open to the changes and willing to take on things that had traditionally been my responsibility in our marriage. He valued our relationship and my health and happiness enough to change his behavior.

My husband began doing things around the house that had always been my responsibility.

He would throw in a load of laundry, unload the dishwasher, stop by the store, and pick up something we needed instead of expecting me to do all of those things. He went to therapy to work on some things that he needed to change.

I set boundaries for the first time in my adult life.

He respected my boundaries

I am very lucky that he realized that the responsibilities in our marriage had been lopsided and was willing to take on more in order to make our marriage work for us both.

I know that not all relationships can survive such a seismic shift. Many of my other friendships and family relationships have floundered or ended, as I have become more comfortable enforcing boundaries.

This shift in my life freed me up to be able to think about myself and what I wanted out of life. We only get one life and we deserve to be happy and fulfilled.

I chose myself and my happiness while still loving my family.

I booked trips I wanted to take. I made plans for things that made me happy. I ended or limited contact with people who would not respect my boundaries. I set limits. I spent the winter before my fiftieth birthday writing the novel I'd always wanted to write. I stopped being responsible for everyone's happiness. I stopped being everyone's caregiver. I stopped thinking the world would stop if I didn't do everything for everyone. I set limits and enforced them.

As I stopped taking responsibility for things that weren't mine to bear, my legs stopped hurting. They didn't feel like someone was holding on and dragging behind me when I walked. My sleep improved. My mental health improved. My marriage improved. People stopped crossing my boundaries when they learned that I would enforce them.

I am happier and more excited about my life than I have ever been.

I want this for you.

You deserve to have an equal partner instead of one that sucks the life out of you.

You deserve not to give your time or energy to toxic people who do not respect your boundaries.

You deserve to chase your own dreams and have the people in your life support us and cheer you on.

I want that for you.

I wrote this book as part of my healing journey. I hope it helps you with yours.

You deserve it.

ARE YOU TAKING REPONSIBILITY FOR THINGS YOU SHOULDN'T?

Sarah woke up earlier than the rest of her household every morning. She made breakfast for her family, helped her kids get ready for school, planned dinner, added items to the grocery list, and then headed off to work. After a long day at the office, she picked up her kids, stopped at the grocery store to get what they needed for dinner, cooked dinner, helped her kids with their homework, and got them ready for bed. By the time she finally had a moment to herself, it was already late at night, she was completely exhausted and she was facing doing it all over again the next day.

Sarah felt like she was doing everything for everyone, but no one was taking responsibility for themselves or caring for her. Her husband often came home late from work, expecting dinner to be on the table and the kids to be ready for bed. Her children constantly demanded her attention and assistance, leaving her with little time to take care of herself.

Even her coworkers relied on her to take on extra projects and work long hours, without offering any support or recognition for her efforts.

Despite her overwhelming workload and lack of support, Sarah felt like she couldn't ask for help or take a break. She didn't want to burden her family or coworkers, and she felt like she needed to keep pushing herself to prove her worth.

But as the weeks and months went by, Sarah's exhaustion and stress began to take a toll on her physical and mental health. She started to have trouble sleeping, experienced constant headaches and body aches, and felt emotionally drained and disconnected from those around her.

Do you relate to Sarah? Do you feel like you're carrying the weight of the world on your shoulders? Do you feel like you're responsible for more than your fair share of the tasks that keep your family running?

It's easy to feel overwhelmed and stressed out when you feel like you're the only one pulling the weight of the tasks of life for your family and in your workplace.

In today's society, there is a lot of pressure on women to be the perfect spouse, parent, and employee. We often find ourselves striving to be everything to everyone. We juggle multiple roles and tasks, both at home and in the workplace, and are expected to excel in all aspects of our lives. It is not uncommon for women to be responsible for cooking, cleaning, laundry, and childcare, all while maintaining a full-time job. This is an unrealistic expectation that society has placed on women.

We constantly juggle multiple responsibilities and become overburdened with too many tasks. This constant juggling can take a toll on our mental and physical health, leading to burnout and stress. This juggling act can have negative consequences on our mental and physical health, resulting in burnout and stress. It's important for us to prioritize our own well-being and take steps to avoid overburdening ourselves.

Managing a household can be overwhelming, especially if you have children or elderly parents to take care of or a spouse who doesn't pull their fair share. We may feel as if we are responsible for everything ourselves, from cooking to cleaning the house. Our partners may expect us to take on all the household tasks, even if we are working full-time, just like they are. This can lead to fatigue, overwhelm, stress, and resentment.

That is what happened to Sarah. She became overwhelmed, exhausted, depressed and was diagnosed with an autoimmune disease and suffered chronic pain. She felt angry and resentful that no one was taking care of her the way she had cared for everyone else around her.

Sarah reached a breaking point. She realized that she couldn't continue to do everything for everyone without taking care of herself first. She started to set boundaries with her family and coworkers, saying no to extra responsibilities and asking for help when she needed it. She also began to prioritize her own self-care, taking time to exercise, meditate, and do things that brought her joy.

As Sarah started to put herself first, she noticed a significant shift in her relationships and overall well-being. Her family and coworkers began to respect her boundaries and offer her more support. She felt more energized and fulfilled in her daily life. Sarah realized that taking care of herself wasn't a selfish act, but rather a necessary step towards being a better mother, wife, coworker, and person.

It's important for us to recognize when we are taking on too much responsibility like Sarah. Also like Sarah, we need to work to set boundaries and take care of ourselves. Saying no when we can't handle more.

Unfortunately, many of us feel guilty saying no or feel like we have to prove ourselves in various aspects of our lives by doing more than everyone else around us. We feel we need to do everything for our family, from housework to childcare to holiday prep. We try to be the perfect wife, mother, daughter, and sister, but it's important to remember that we can't do it all.

In the workplace, we are often expected to take on tasks that are not part of our job description. We are asked to organize office parties, take on extra projects, and cover for absent colleagues, all while trying to meet our own deadlines and responsibilities.

We are expected to be everything to everyone, and it can be exhausting. Once we have recognized that we are taking on responsibilities that are not ours to bear, we can set healthy boundaries. We can recognize that we can't do it all and that asking for help is not a sign of weakness.

Delegating tasks and responsibilities to others is crucial. Trusting others to do their job efficiently allows us to focus on our own tasks and perform better. This means saying no when we need to and not feeling guilty about it. It means recognizing that we are responsible for our own happiness and well-being and that we cannot control the actions or emotions of others. By doing these things, we can avoid burnout and keep our productivity levels high.

Communication is key in any relationship, and if your husband is not pulling his weight at home, it's important to have an honest and open conversation with him. Let him know how you're feeling and explain how his actions (or lack thereof) are affecting you and your family. Explain to him how you're feeling and the impact that his lack of involvement is having on you and the family. It's possible that he may not realize the extent of your frustration and exhaustion. Be specific about what tasks you need help with and come up with a plan together to divide the responsibilities fairly.

Ideally, when you talk to your husband about how you are feeling, he will agree to take on some of the responsibilities for himself.

But not all partners are willing.

Having a husband who refuses to take on his share of the responsibilities can be frustrating and exhausting.

If your partner is resistant to helping out, it may be time to re-evaluate your family dynamic. It is not okay to do all of the caretaking in your family and not get taken care of in return. It is not okay for one person to bear the brunt of the responsibilities in a relationship.

This may be a sign that you are in a codependent or toxic relationship.

In a toxic or codependent relationship, it's easy to fall into the trap of trying to solve problems that aren't our responsibility. We may feel a deep sense of obligation to ensure our partner's happiness, mental health, and overall success in life.

When we find ourselves in a toxic or codependent relationship, we often take on more responsibility than we should. Yet, this can quickly spiral into a cycle of co-dependency, where our needs and desires take a backseat to our partner's issues.

As we begin to feel increasingly resentful and frustrated towards our partner, we may feel that we're being taken advantage of. This can create a toxic dynamic where we're constantly sacrificing ourselves for the benefit of our partner. The end result is often exhaustion, emotional turmoil, and even physical illness. It's crucial to recognize the signs of co-dependency early on and take steps to address these issues before they spiral out of control.

Consider seeking the help of a therapist or counselor to work through the underlying issues and communication barriers that may be contributing to the problem. Many other women are dealing with the same issues, and there is no shame in asking for help or seeking support.

A Meditation for Letting Go of Things That Aren't My Responsibility

*F*ind a comfortable seated position, close your eyes, and take a deep breath in through your nose.

Hold it for a moment and then exhale slowly through your mouth.

Repeat this a few times until you feel centered and calm.

Visualize yourself standing on the edge of a cliff, overlooking a vast ocean.

The sun is setting, casting a warm glow over the water.

Take a deep breath in, and as you exhale, imagine yourself releasing any thoughts or emotions that are weighing you down.

Now, bring to mind something that you have been holding onto that is not your responsibility.

Perhaps it is a friend's problem that you feel guilty for not being able to solve, or a family member's illness that you cannot control.

Whatever it may be, acknowledge it and hold it in your mind's eye.

As you continue to breathe deeply, imagine yourself holding this burden in your hands.

Visualize the weight of it and notice how it feels in your body.

Now, say to yourself, "I release this burden. It is not mine to carry."

As you exhale, let go of the burden, allowing it to fall away from you and disappear into the ocean. Watch it as it drifts further and further away until it is no longer visible.

Feel the weight lifting from your shoulders, and the relief that comes with letting go.

Now, imagine yourself standing in the middle of a beautiful, peaceful garden. Lush greenery, colorful flowers, and the sound of birds singing in the distance surround you.

As you look around, you notice that there are several heavy bags and boxes scattered around the garden.

These bags and boxes represent the worries, fears, and responsibilities that you have been carrying with you.

They are not yours to bear, but you have been holding onto them, anyway.

Take a moment to observe these bags and boxes.

Notice how heavy they are and how much they are weighing you down.

But also notice that they are separate from you.

They are not a part of who you are.

Now, take a deep breath in and imagine yourself reaching out to one of these bags. As you do, imagine that you are releasing it from your grip.

Feel the weight of it leaving your hands and falling to the

ground.

As you release the bag, repeat the following affirmations to yourself:

"I release this burden. It is not mine to bear."

"I let go of the things that are not my responsibility."

"I am free from the weight of these worries and fears."

Repeat these affirmations as many times as you need to fully let go of the bag.

Then, take a deep breath in and exhale slowly through your mouth.

Repeat this process with each of the bags and boxes in the garden.

With each release, repeat the affirmations to yourself and feel the weight lifting from your shoulders.

As you release each bag, notice how much lighter you feel.

Notice how much more peaceful and relaxed you become. And notice that you are creating space for more positive things to enter your life.

When you have released all the bags and boxes, take a moment to bask in the garden's peacefulness.

Take a deep breath in and exhale slowly through your mouth.

When you are ready, slowly open your eyes and return to the present moment.

ACCEPTING LIMITATIONS OF RESPONSIBILITY

We are constantly bombarded with messages that tell us we should be in control of everything, and that we should be able to achieve anything we set our minds to. While it is important to set goals and work towards them, it is equally important to recognize when something is outside of our control. Learning to accept our limitations can be a difficult process, but it is essential for our mental health and well-being.

We all want to be in control of our lives. We want to handle everything that comes our way and be responsible for every aspect of our lives.

However, this is an impossible feat. There will always be

things that are beyond our control.

Accepting our limitations is not a sign of weakness, but a sign of strength. It is an acknowledgment of the reality that we cannot control everything, and that it is okay.

We must recognize that we are not responsible for everything. We have a limited amount of control over our own lives and actions, and even that is not absolute. We cannot control the actions of others, and we cannot control external factors that impact our lives.

Once we accept this, we can let go of the need for control. This can be a difficult process, as it often means confronting our own fears and insecurities. We may fear failure, rejection, the loss of control, or we may simply feel uncomfortable with uncertainty.

To overcome these fears, we must learn to trust ourselves and our abilities. We must recognize that we can handle whatever comes our way, even if it's not what we would have chosen. Failure is a natural part of the learning process, rather than a reflection of our worth as individuals. When we try to control things that are outside of our control, we set ourselves up for disappointment and frustration.

By acknowledging that we are not solely responsible for every outcome, we open ourselves up to appreciate the contributions of others. This appreciation can lead to stronger relationships and a greater sense of community. Attempting to control everything in our lives can lead to stress, anxiety, and burnout. Recognizing when something is outside of our control allows us to focus our energy on things that we can control and to let go of things that we cannot. This shift in focus can help us feel more empowered and in control of our lives.

Recognizing our limitations and accepting them is crucial for leading a fulfilling life. Whether it's physical, mental, or emotional, we all have areas where we fall short. By recognizing and accepting our limitations, we can redirect our focus toward the things we can control
and work towards personal growth.

By understanding what is within our power and what isn't, we can focus on the things that matter most. It's easy to get caught up in worrying about things that are beyond our control, but by recognizing our limitations, we can shift our focus to what we can control and make a positive impact on our lives.

By accepting our limitations, we can shift our focus to things that we can actually do something about. This can help us feel more empowered and in control of our lives and lead to greater self-awareness and self-compassion.

When we try to take on too much or push ourselves beyond our limits, we can end up feeling frustrated and disappointed in ourselves. By recognizing our limitations and being kind to ourselves when we fall short, we can cultivate self-acceptance and self-love.

When we learn to accept the limitations of our responsibility, we feel less stressed and anxious. We let go of the things that are not within our responsibilities and focus on the things that are actually our responsibility. We'll be able to focus our energy on the things that matter, and this can help us be more productive.

When you recognize your limitations, you'll gain a better understanding of yourself. You'll be able to identify your strengths and weaknesses, and this can help you make better decisions in your personal and professional life.

Learning to accept your limitations can also improve your relationships with others. When you try to take on too much or feel responsible for things that are not your burden, you can become resentful and overwhelmed. By setting clear boundaries and recognizing when you need to say "no," you can have more fulfilling and harmonious relationships with those around you.

Here are a few strategies to help in accepting the limitations of responsibility:

Practice self-compassion. When you find yourself falling short or making mistakes, be kind to yourself. Treat yourself with the same compassion and understanding that you would offer a friend in a similar situation.

Be honest with yourself about what you can realistically accomplish. Don't set yourself up for failure by taking on too much or trying to be perfect. Instead of worrying about things that are outside of your control, focus on the things that you can actually do something about.

Set boundaries and be willing to say "no" when something is not a good fit for you or when you simply don't have the time or energy to take it on. We'll go into much greater detail on boundaries in a future chapter.

Remember that nobody is perfect and that it's okay to make mistakes. Embrace your imperfections and celebrate your strengths.

Learning to accept our limitations is not always easy, but it is an important step toward leading a fulfilling and meaningful life. By recognizing what is within our control and what is beyond it, we can focus our energy on what truly matters and cultivate a greater sense of self-awareness and self-compassion. So the next time you struggle with a limitation, remember that it's okay to fall short, and that acceptance is a powerful tool for personal growth and happiness.

A Meditation: I Am Not Responsible for Fixing Everything for Everyone

Find a quiet and comfortable place to sit.

Take a few deep breaths and allow your mind to settle.

Repeat the following mantra to yourself: "I am not responsible for fixing everything for everyone."

Visualize a burden or weight that you have been carrying. See it as a heavy backpack that you have been lugging around.

Visualize yourself unzipping the backpack and taking out the burden. See it as a separate object that is no longer attached to you.

Hold the burden in your hand and acknowledge it for what it is. Recognize that it is not yours to carry.

Take a deep breath and release the burden. See it floating away from you, becoming smaller and smaller until it disappears.

Repeat the mantra again: "I am not responsible for fixing everything for everyone."

Sit in stillness for a few more moments, allowing yourself to feel the lightness of no longer carrying this burden.

BUT I HAVE TO.....

Do you feel as if you are the only person who can do the things for everyone that you do? Do you take pride in being selfless and putting everyone else's needs above your own?

As human beings, it's natural for us to want to care for those who depend on us. Be it our children, our spouses, our friends, our coworkers, or our aging parents, we take pride in ensuring their well-being and happiness. Putting others first and caring for members of our community has helped us survive and thrive as social creatures.

But feeling responsible for everyone and everything in our sphere can crossover into people-pleasing, martyrdom, and enabling. We become "people-pleasers" and end up taking on more than our fair share of responsibilities, obligations, and tasks.

As someone who has struggled with people-pleasing and a hyper sense of responsibility, I have often found myself on the verge of martyrdom. I have given up my own needs and desires for the sake of my loved one, thinking that this was the right thing to do. But over time, I have come to realize that this mindset is not healthy, and it is not sustainable.

There are many reasons why someone might become a people pleaser and hyper-responsible. Perhaps you grew up in a household where you were expected to put others' needs before your own. Maybe you were rewarded for being helpful and accommodating, and so you learned that this was the best way to get approval and validation from others. Or, it could be that you have a deep-seated fear of rejection or abandonment, and you believe that being a people pleaser is the only way to keep the people you care about in your life.

Whatever the reason, the end result is the same: you end up taking on more than your fair share of responsibilities and obligations. You may find yourself saying "yes" to things you don't really want to do, or taking on extra work because you don't want to let anyone down. Over time, this can lead to resentment, burnout, and martyrdom.

We often hear stories of individuals who gave up their dreams to support someone else's or to care for another person being relayed with awe from the person telling the story. While sacrifice and selflessness are admirable qualities, being a martyr is not something that we should aspire to be.

It is important to understand that martyrdom is not a solution to our problems, nor is it a means to achieve our goals.

In fact, it's detrimental to us and to the people we care about.

Many people view martyrs as heroes. However, in reality, martyrdom is often a result of a lack of self-care and boundaries.

If you feel that you have to do everything for your loved ones or everyone's world will crash around you, it is time to reevaluate.

Make a list of everything you need to do and then rank them in order of importance. Focus on the most important tasks first and then move on to the less important ones. This will help you feel more in control of your responsibilities and prevent you from feeling like you're drowning in tasks. Then, think about which tasks could be done by someone else. Maybe your spouse can take on some of the daily household chores, or your children can help with meal preparation.

In most cases, there are tasks that can be delegated to others. Talk to your colleagues or family members and see what tasks they will take on. Delegating tasks will help you focus on the most important responsibilities and prevent you from feeling like you have to do everything yourself. It's also a way to encourage others to step up and take on some responsibilities.

Your loved ones or co-workers may not even realize that you are struggling or that you need help. It's important to communicate clearly and respectfully with those around you and let them know you need their help.

For example, if you're feeling overwhelmed with work, it's okay to let your boss know you can't take on any additional projects at the moment. Often, people will step up and take on some responsibilities, but they may not know that you need their help if you don't tell them.

Are there boundaries that you need to set?

It's essential to set boundaries and stick to them. This can mean saying "no" to certain tasks or taking a break when you need it. By setting boundaries, you can avoid burnout and ensure that you have the energy to continue caring for your loved ones.

Now, setting boundaries and delegating tasks can be easier said than done. Many of us feel guilty for doing so. It's important to remember that setting boundaries and delegating tasks is not a sign of weakness, it's a sign of strength and self-awareness.

It's okay to say no to certain requests or to set limits on how much you can do. Your world will not crash and burn if you set a limit. I promise!

In fact, setting boundaries and delegating tasks can be an act of self-care. It's a way to ensure that we don't become overwhelmed and burnt out. By taking care of yourself, you can better take care of those around you.

Take care of your physical and emotional needs by eating healthy, getting enough sleep, and practicing mindfulness. Self-care will help you manage your stress and prevent burnout. Taking care of yourself is important, especially when you're feeling overwhelmed and exhausted. When you feel you absolutely do not have time to take a break or perform self-care, that is when you need to do it the most. Step away from your responsibilities for a little while and do something that relaxes you. Taking a break will help you recharge and come back to your responsibilities with a fresh perspective.

There are certain circumstances where delegation and setting boundaries may not be possible. For example, if you have a disabled child or spouse, and no one is around to help, then you may need to take on all the responsibilities by yourself. However, there are steps you can take to manage your stress and regain control of your life even in situations like this. You may not have anyone who can help you care for your child, but maybe you can order healthy nourishing meals through a meal service or take short breaks scattered throughout the day when you can practice meditation, deep breathing, or go for a walk, even if it is just out to the mailbox and back.

Talk to friends, family, or a professional if you're feeling stressed or anxious. Sometimes talking to someone can help you see things from a different perspective and give you the support you need. If you're feeling overwhelmed and don't feel you have any options, it may be time to seek support from a professional. There's no shame in asking for help when you need it.

A Meditation: It Is Not My Responsibility to Rescue Everyone

Sit in a comfortable position with your spine straight and your eyes closed.

Take a deep breath in and release it slowly.

As you inhale, feel the air fill your lungs and expand your belly.

As you exhale, release any tension or stress in your body.

Allow yourself to sink deeper into a state of relaxation with each breath.

Now, bring to mind someone in your life who you have been trying to rescue. Perhaps it is a friend who is going through a difficult time, a family member who is struggling with addiction, or a partner who is dealing with mental health issues.

Visualize them in your mind's eye and notice any feelings that arise in your body as you think of them.

As you continue to breathe deeply, repeat the following affirmations to yourself:

"It is not my responsibility to rescue everyone."

"I trust each person is on their own path and will find their own way."

"I release any guilt or shame I have been carrying for not being able to fix everything."

"I honor the boundaries of others and respect their autonomy."

"I am grateful for the opportunity to offer support and guidance when I can, but I know that ultimately, each person is responsible for their own healing."

Allow these affirmations to sink in and repeat them as many times as you need to. As you do so, visualize a weight being lifted off your shoulders.

Repeat this a few times until you feel calm and centered.

Now, visualize a beautiful garden in front of you.

This garden represents your inner self.

Take a few moments to observe the garden.

Notice the colors, the textures, and the scents.

As you look around, you notice a tree in the center of the garden.

This tree represents you.

Take a few moments to observe the tree.

Notice its height, its branches, and its leaves.

Now, imagine that there are birds perched on the branches of the tree. These birds represent the people in your life that you want to help.

Take a few moments to observe the birds. Notice their colors, their sizes, and their movements.

As you watch the birds, you notice that one of them is caught in a vine.

This bird represents someone in your life that you feel the need to rescue.

Take a few moments to observe the bird.

Now, repeat the following affirmation to yourself: "It is not my responsibility to rescue everyone. I am not selfish for taking care of myself first. I respect my boundaries and limitations."

As you say this affirmation, visualize the bird freeing itself from the vine, flying away from the tree, and out of the garden.

Watch as it disappears into the distance, and notice how you feel lighter and more at peace.

Take a few moments to sit with this feeling of peace and remind yourself that it is not your responsibility to rescue everyone.

You have your own limitations, and it is crucial to take care of yourself first.

When you are ready, slowly open your eyes and return to the present moment.

SETTING HEALTHY BOUNDARIES AND THE POWER OF NO

As a partner, wife, and/or mother, it's easy to fall into the trap of taking on everything that comes your way. From working and managing the household to taking care of the kids and your spouse, it can be very overwhelming. But it's important to remember that you are not responsible for everything and that setting boundaries is crucial for your mental and emotional well-being.

Boundaries are the lines that we draw around ourselves to protect our physical, emotional, and mental well-being. They are the limits that we set for ourselves and others to ensure that we are not overextending ourselves, taking on too much, or being taken advantage of.

Boundaries are essential for maintaining a healthy relationship with ourselves and others. When these boundaries are not established or enforced, the repercussions can be far-reaching and have negative impacts on our physical, emotional, and mental health.

Setting boundaries can be difficult, especially for those who have a history of people-pleasing, people who have a hard time saying no, or people in toxic or abusive relationships. A lack of healthy boundaries can lead to codependency in relationships. Codependency is a pattern of behavior where we rely on other people to fulfill our emotional or physical needs. This can manifest in a variety of ways, such as always putting others' needs before our own, seeking approval and validation from others, and feeling responsible for other people's feelings or behaviors. Codependency can damage our relationships, our self-esteem, and our mental health.

When we don't set healthy boundaries, it can also lead to a range of negative repercussions that can affect our physical, emotional, and mental well-being.

One of the most significant repercussions of not setting healthy boundaries is chronic stress. When we don't set boundaries, we can become overwhelmed and over-committed, leading to stress and anxiety.

Chronic stress can have a detrimental effect on our physical and mental health, leading to a range of problems, such as high blood pressure, heart disease, depression, and anxiety.

Another repercussion of not setting healthy boundaries is resentment. When we don't set boundaries, we can become resentful and angry with our partners, friends, and family members. It's important to communicate our feelings and needs clearly to avoid feeling resentful towards others. It's important to remember that our partners and loved ones can't do better if they don't know how we are feeling. This can create a cycle of passive-aggressive behavior and cause rifts in our relationships.

When we don't set limits on our time, energy, and resources, we can become over-committed and overwhelmed. This can lead to physical and emotional exhaustion, which can ultimately result in burnout. Burnout can impact every aspect of our lives, from our work to our relationships and our mental health. It can also lead to feelings of hopelessness and depression.

Inflammation is another negative consequence of not setting healthy boundaries. When our bodies are under stress, they release inflammatory markers to help fight off perceived threats. However, when this response is chronic, it can lead to long-term inflammation, which can damage our organs and tissues and increase our risk of chronic disease. Inflammation can cause a range of health problems, such as arthritis, heart disease, cancer, and autoimmune diseases. When we don't set healthy boundaries, we can become so stressed and anxious that it can affect our immune system, leading to the development of autoimmune diseases.

Without boundaries, we may feel guilty for taking time for ourselves or feel like we don't have the time to prioritize self-care. Self-care is critical for our overall well-being, and it involves taking time for ourselves to rest, recharge, and engage in activities that bring us joy. This can lead to feelings of resentment, frustration, and burnout.

Setting boundaries is an essential aspect of self-respect, and when we don't prioritize our own needs, we can feel like we don't deserve to be treated with respect. It's essential to establish clear expectations and limits on our time, energy, and emotional investment. By doing so, we can prevent burnout, prioritize self-care, prevent codependency, and boost our self-esteem.

Setting boundaries is not always easy, but it's a necessary step toward living a healthy, balanced life.

So the question is, how do we go about changing our ingrained patterns of behavior and start setting healthy boundaries with people who are used to us being a certain way?

As social creatures, it's natural to want to please those around us and make them happy. However, there comes a point when we need to prioritize our own well-being and establish healthy boundaries with others, especially when dealing with people who take advantage of us because we pick up the slack when they don't pull their weight.

This can be especially challenging when dealing with people who have become accustomed to our previous behaviors and may not react positively to these changes.

The first step to setting healthy boundaries is knowing what they are. Take some time to reflect on what behaviors or actions from others make you feel uncomfortable or disrespected. From there, you can decide what boundaries you need to set with those specific people.

It is also important to know your limits. This means understanding your physical, emotional, and mental capacities and recognizing when you are reaching your limits. It is essential to listen to your body and your emotions and to take steps to ensure that you are not pushing yourself too hard.

For example, if you know you need eight hours of sleep to function at your best, make sure that you prioritize getting enough rest each night. If someone in your life doesn't respect your need for sleep, clearly set the boundary of when you expect to be left alone to seel and how to handle it if they want something from you during your rest time.

If you find that spending too much time with a particular person drains your energy, limit your time with them or find ways to protect yourself while you are around them.

Make a list of all the things you are responsible for in your household, at work, and with your family. Write down all the tasks you do in a week and look at which ones you are the only person who can do them, and which ones you can delegate to someone else. This could include things like cooking meals, doing laundry, taking care of the kids, paying bills, and so on.

Once you have a clear understanding of your responsibilities, you can start to set boundaries around them.

It is essential to recognize when you are feeling overwhelmed, stressed, or anxious and to take the necessary steps to address those feelings. Knowing your limits also means recognizing when you need to take a break or step back from a situation. For example, if you are feeling overwhelmed at work, it may be time to take a vacation or a mental health day. Recognizing your limits and taking the steps to care for yourself is essential to setting healthy boundaries.

Learning to say no is a crucial aspect of setting healthy boundaries. Saying no can be difficult, especially if you have a history of people-pleasing. However, saying no is essential to protecting your well-being and maintaining healthy boundaries. When saying no, it is important to be clear and direct. You do not need to provide an explanation or justification for your decision. Simply saying no is enough.

Another important aspect of setting healthy boundaries is identifying what you can and cannot control. We often waste energy trying to control things that are beyond our control, which can lead to frustration and burnout. It is important to recognize what we can control and focus our efforts on those areas. For example, you cannot control how other people behave or react to situations. You can only control your own reactions and behavior. By focusing on what you can control, you can set healthy boundaries and protect your well-being.

Once you've identified your boundaries, it's important to communicate them clearly and directly to the people involved. Be honest and upfront about what you need from them and why it's important to you. Avoid being confrontational or aggressive, but stand firm in your boundaries.

Setting boundaries is only effective if you're consistent in enforcing them. Be prepared for push-back from people who may be used to your previous behavior, but don't give in. Stick to your boundaries and don't compromise your well-being. If you let someone cross a boundary that you have set, they will not respect your boundaries in the future.

Think of a toddler asking for a snack. If you say no five times but give them the snack, the sixth time they ask for it, you have just trained your toddler to harass you until you cave and give them what they want. The same thing holds true for boundary crossers.

Changing ingrained patterns of behavior can be difficult, and it's okay to seek support from friends, family, or even a therapist. Surround yourself with people who respect your boundaries and understand why they're important to you.

A Meditation on Setting Boundaries

F ind a quiet and comfortable place where you won't be disturbed.

Sit down and take a few deep breaths, allowing yourself to relax and let go of any tension or stress.

Slowly count backward from ten to one. As you count, go deeper into a state of mediation.

10

9

8

7

6

5

4

3

2

1

Now, bring to mind a situation where you felt your boundaries were crossed. It could be a recent event or something from your past.

Visualize the situation in your mind and notice how it makes you feel.

Do you feel angry, frustrated, sad, or overwhelmed?

Allow yourself to experience these emotions without judgment. Just observe them and let them be.

Now, imagine yourself surrounded by a bubble of protective energy. This energy represents your boundaries. See it as a strong and impenetrable shield that keeps you safe and protected.

Take a moment to feel the strength and power of this energy.

As you sit within your bubble of energy, repeat these affirmations to yourself:

"I am worthy of respect and kindness."

"I deserve to have my needs and boundaries respected."

"I have the power to set healthy boundaries and protect myself."

"I trust myself to know what's best for me."

Take a few deep breaths and allow these affirmations to sink in.

Feel the strength and confidence that comes from knowing you are worthy and deserving of respect and boundaries.

Now, imagine yourself in a future situation where you need to set a boundary.

Visualize yourself communicating your needs clearly and assertively, without fear or hesitation.

See the other person respecting your boundaries and responding positively.

Take a moment to feel the sense of empowerment and peace that comes from setting healthy boundaries.

Finally, take a few more deep breaths and return to the present moment.

WHY DO WE DO THIS?

Have you ever wondered why you find yourself doing more than your fair share, even when it's harmful to your own well-being? Why do you feel responsible for everything and everyone? Why you do feel the need to please others?

There are many reasons we may fall into the trap of hyper-responsibility and constantly trying to please others.

We might feel like we will be rejected if we don't do everything for everyone. We might believe that if we don't do everything, people won't like us or won't find us valuable. This fear of rejection can be a powerful motivator, and it can drive us to do things we wouldn't normally do. Our self-worth may also be tied up in being indispensable. We may think that our worth is determined by how much we can do for others.

Another reason is the desire for acceptance. We might feel like we need to prove ourselves to others in order to be accepted. We might believe that if we don't go above and beyond, we won't be accepted. This can lead to a vicious cycle of over-commitment and burnout. This desire for acceptance can be fueled by our need for validation and can lead us to do things we don't really want to do.

Our self-worth can also be tied up with being indispensable. We might feel like we need to be needed in order to feel good about ourselves.

Some of us might also be fiercely loyal. We might feel like we need to take on others' responsibilities because we care about them deeply. We might believe that if we don't do everything, we're letting them down. This loyalty can be admirable, but it can also lead to exhaustion and resentment.

For some of us, the need to be strong is tied to those around us being wounded or weak. We might feel like we need to be the 'strong one' because they can't take care of themselves. This can be a heavy burden to carry.

Empathy can also play a role in our tendency to do everything for everyone. We might feel the pain of others deeply and want to do everything we can to help them. We might believe that if we don't do everything, we're failing our loved ones. This can lead to a sense of guilt and a feeling that we're not doing enough. Being highly empathic often comes from being raised in a situation where it isn't safe to express ourselves. We become highly sensitive to the emotions of those around us, always on alert for danger.

Only children and firstborn children often feel like they need to take care of everyone. Firstborns and only children are often raised to be responsible and to take care of themselves and others at a young age. This can lead to a sense of obligation and a feeling that they need to be the ones to take care of everything. This can be a positive trait, but it can also lead to feeling like you are responsible for everyone and everything.

If we were raised by narcissistic or abusive parents, we might have learned that our worth is tied up in being needed by others.

In our quest to appease our parents, we might have learned that we need to do everything we can to please them and avoid their wrath. We may have learned to prioritize their needs over our own. We may feel that our worth is determined by how much we can do for others and that we are not important unless we are pleasing someone else.

My mother was abused as a child. I knew about her abuse as a very young child. As an only child, there was very little separation between my parents and myself. They had adult conversations about her abuse that should have been kept away from me at five years old. I was told by my father that I was strong like him and that my mom was delicate. That it was our job to protect her.

I felt responsible for protecting her and caring for her at an age when she was actually responsible for protecting and caring for me. I was constantly on alert due to my mother's erratic behavior. This set me up for a lifetime of taking on responsibilities for things that aren't mine to take on and for feeling like I needed to protect and care for everyone around me. It set me up for a lifetime of codependent, unhealthy, and toxic relationships.

Being raised by disordered or abusive parents can make us vulnerable to manipulative and controlling individuals who prey on our desire to please others and our empathy.

This can set us up to be victims of narcissists and abusers in future relationships, as we have learned to prioritize the needs of others over our own.

Children from dysfunctional families are often forced to grow up quickly, taking on responsibilities that are beyond their years. They may become the caretakers or the emotional support for their parents or siblings.

As a result, children from dysfunctional families learn to be hyper-aware of their surroundings and the emotions of those around them. They become attuned to the needs of others, often at the expense of their own needs. These children learn to anticipate the moods and behaviors of others in an attempt to avoid conflict or to protect themselves from harm. They become skilled at reading body language, tone of voice, and facial expressions.

Children from dysfunctional families often become empaths. Empaths have a heightened sensitivity to the emotions of others. Empaths are compassionate, caring, and empathetic. They can sense and absorb the emotions of others, sometimes to the point where they feel overwhelmed. Empaths can feel the emotions of others as if they were their own. Empaths are deeply attuned to the energy of those around them and can often sense when something is wrong, even if the other person is not expressing it verbally. They have an innate ability to offer comfort, support, and understanding to those who are going through a difficult time. Empaths have the unique ability to understand and feel the emotions of others, are highly intuitive, and can sense the energy of those around them.

Empaths have often been through adversity and have learned to navigate complex emotional situations.

While this can be a gift in many ways, it can also set them up for being in a toxic or abusive relationship. The empath may feel responsible for the other person's happiness, even if it means sacrificing their own.

Empaths are vulnerable to becoming enmeshed in relationships where they take on too much responsibility for the other person's emotions and behaviors.

A pattern of codependency can develop where they become overly invested in the other person's life and well-being. They may neglect their own needs and desires in order to meet the needs of the other person.

This can be emotionally draining and can lead to feelings of resentment or anger over time.

The empaths' ability to feel the emotions of others can make it difficult to set boundaries in relationships. They may feel like they are responsible for the other person's emotions and behavior, and may struggle to assert their own needs and desires.

This can leave them feeling powerless and vulnerable in the relationship.

Empaths are often drawn to people who are in pain or suffering and feel a powerful urge to help them. They have a deep desire to make things better for others, even if it means sacrificing their own well-being.

Empaths often attract narcissists or other toxic individuals. Abusers seek out empaths because they sense that they are more likely to tolerate their behavior. The empath may feel like they are responsible for the abuser's happiness and will go to great lengths to try to make them feel better, even if it means sacrificing their own well-being. Narcissists are drawn to empaths because they sense their caring nature and ability to empathize. They see empaths as easy targets for manipulation and control. Empaths are often too kind and understanding to see the red flags in these relationships until it's too late.

Empaths are often the children of narcissists or abusers, so those relationships and patterns of behavior feel familiar and can be mistaken for love.

In a toxic or abusive relationship, the abuser may manipulate empaths into feeling responsible for their happiness or well-being. They may use guilt or other tactics to make them feel like they are the only ones who can help them.

It's important to recognize that this type of behavior is not healthy, and it's essential to set boundaries in your relationships.

If you find yourself constantly taking on the emotional burden of others, it's time to take a step back and evaluate the situation. Ask yourself if the relationship is truly healthy and if you are receiving as much as you are giving. No relationship is 50/50 all the time but if your relationship is always heavily weighed toward your partner, it is not healthy.

If you recognize these patterns in your own relationships, it's important to take steps to protect your own well-being. This may involve setting boundaries with the other person, seeking support from friends or family members, or seeking professional help.

Learn to say no and prioritize your own needs.
Be aware of the red flags in relationships.
Trust your intuition and recognize when someone is trying to manipulate or control you.
Look for partners who are supportive and understanding and don't take advantage of you.
Recognize when you are taking on too much responsibility for someone else's emotions or behavior and take a step back.
Remember, you are not responsible for the emotions or behavior of others.
It is okay to say no and set boundaries.

We do not have to do everything for everyone, and it is not our responsibility to fix everyone's problems or manage everyone's emotions. It is important to prioritize our own well-being and take care of ourselves.

We can still be kind and empathic while also taking care of ourselves.

Remember that your emotional well-being is just as important as anyone else's, and don't be afraid to say no. By taking care of yourself, you'll be better equipped to help others in a healthy and sustainable way.

A Meditation on Overcoming Codependence

Close your eyes and take a few deep breaths, inhaling through your nose and exhaling through your mouth.

With each breath, feel yourself becoming more relaxed and more centered.

As you settle into your breath, bring to mind an image of yourself.

See yourself standing tall, with a bright light shining from within you.

This light represents your inner strength and resilience.

Now, bring to mind an image of someone you've been codependent with. This could be a partner, a family member, or a friend. See yourself with that person and observe your feelings without judgment. Allow yourself to feel these emotions, but don't dwell on them.

As you see them in your mind's eye, notice any feelings that arise. You might feel anger, frustration, sadness, or a sense of longing. Without judging yourself or the other person, simply observe these emotions.

Allow them to be there without trying to push them away or cling to them.

As you continue to breathe deeply, imagine a cord connecting you to the other person. This cord represents the energetic attachment that has kept you bound together. Notice the color and texture of the cord, and observe any sensations in your body that arise as you focus on it.

Now, imagine that you're holding a pair of scissors.

With each exhale, imagine yourself snipping away a piece of the cord. As you cut away the cord, feel a sense of release and freedom.

Know that you're not cutting off your love or compassion for the other person, but simply releasing the unhealthy attachment that has kept you stuck.

With each breath, continue cutting away pieces of the cord until it's completely severed.

As you do so, imagine the other person being bathed in a warm, healing light. Know that they're capable of healing and growing, just as you are.

Imagine yourself standing in front of a mirror.

Look deeply into your own eyes and repeat the following affirmations to yourself:

"I am worthy of love and respect."

"I am capable of making my own decisions."

"I am responsible for my own happiness."

Feel the power of these affirmations as you repeat them. Allow yourself to let go of the need for external validation and trust in your own worth and capabilities.

As you continue to breathe deeply, focus on the light surrounding you. See it growing stronger and brighter, filling you with love and empowerment.

Imagine yourself with the person who triggers your codependency once again.

This time, see yourself standing tall and strong, with the light of self-love shining brightly within you. See yourself responding to the person with confidence and assertiveness, knowing that you are capable of making your own decisions and taking care of yourself.

Finally, bring your attention back to yourself. See yourself standing tall and strong, with a sense of inner peace and clarity. Know that you're capable of creating healthy relationships and of loving and caring for yourself.

Take a few more deep breaths, and when you're ready, gently open your eyes.

RECOGNIZING NARCISSISTS AND OTHER TOXIC PEOPLE

Are you in a relationship or friendship with someone who makes you feel like you are walking on eggshells around them? Does this person make everything about themselves and doesn't give you the attention or care you deserve? Do you feel drained, frustrated, like a failure or confused after interacting with them?

You may be dealing with someone who is narcissistic.

Everyone has some narcissism but when it is extreme, it can be very damaging to the people they are in relationships with. In some cases, a person may have Narcissistic Personality Disorder. NPD is a personality disorder characterized by a grandiose sense of self-importance, a lack of empathy, and a need for admiration. Narcissists believe they are special, entitled to special treatment, and often lack empathy for others.

Narcissists have a grandiose view of themselves and may exaggerate their accomplishments or abilities. They may also have a sense of entitlement and expect others to cater to their needs.

One common trait of a narcissist is their need for attention and admiration. They can often come across as charming and charismatic, but their intentions are self-serving. They may manipulate others to get what they want and lack empathy for others. If someone consistently puts their own needs above others, it may be a sign that they have narcissistic tendencies.

Another characteristic of a narcissist is their tendency to criticize or belittle others. They may frequently make negative comments about others and try to bring them down to make themselves feel superior. This behavior can be harmful and cause those around them to feel insecure and anxious.

It's important to pay attention to how a person treats others. If someone consistently puts others down or makes them feel inferior, it may be a sign that they have a personality disorder or a toxic personality. However, it's important not to jump to conclusions and make assumptions about someone's behavior. It's important to consider the context of the situation and the individual's behavior over time.

So, how can you recognize a narcissist?

Here are some signs to look out for:

1. Grandiosity: A narcissist often has an exaggerated sense of self-importance and expects admiration from others. They

may exaggerate their accomplishments or abilities.

2. Lack of empathy: Narcissists often struggle to understand or care about the feelings of others.

3. Entitlement: They have a sense of entitlement and believe they deserve special treatment. They may feel entitled to special treatment or privileges, even if they haven't earned it.

4. Manipulation: They are often manipulative and will use others to achieve their goals. Narcissists often use others for their own gain, manipulating and exploiting them to get what they want.

5. Arrogance: Narcissists may come across as overly confident or arrogant, which can turn people off.

6. Need for attention: They may crave attention and admiration, often at the expense of others.

7. Inability to accept criticism: Narcissists may become defensive or angry when criticized, even if the criticism is constructive.

8. Lack of accountability: They may refuse to take responsibility for their actions and blame others for their mistakes.

9. Jealousy: Narcissists may be overly jealous of others who they perceive as a threat to their ego.

10. Self-centeredness: They are preoccupied with themselves and their own needs, often at the expense of others.

11. Unstable Relationships: They may have a history of unstable relationships and may struggle to maintain long-term connections.

12. Love bombing: They may overwhelm you with attention early in the relationship and rush you into a serious relationship

or marriage very quickly before you catch on to their behavior.

It's essential to understand that Narcissists and other toxic people are not always easy to identify. They can be charming and charismatic, and they know how to manipulate and control others.

Toxic individuals often have low self-esteem and seek validation and attention from others and may use emotional blackmail or passive-aggressive behavior to get what they want. They often lack empathy and consideration for others. They may try to control every aspect of your life, from the way you dress to the people you spend time with. They might also make you feel guilty or ashamed for having a different opinion or for not complying with their demands.

One strategy for dealing with these types of people is called "grey rocking."

Grey rocking is a technique that involves becoming as uninteresting and unresponsive as possible when interacting with a narcissist or toxic person. You work to become emotionally detached and unresponsive when interacting with them. The goal is to give them as little emotional reaction or attention as possible, essentially making oneself as "boring" or uninteresting as a grey rock.

This approach is based on the idea that these individuals thrive on drama, attention, and emotional reactions. By reducing the amount of emotional fuel you provide, you can starve them of the attention they crave. Narcissists seek to control and manipulate others by provoking emotional reactions and creating chaos. By using the grey rocking technique, you deny them the emotional reactions they crave, and they quickly lose interest in you. This makes you less of a target for their manipulations, and they may eventually move on to someone else who is more willing to engage with their drama.

There are several benefits to using the grey rocking technique.

First, it can help you remain calm and composed in situations that would otherwise be emotionally charged. This can be incredibly helpful when dealing with someone who is trying to provoke you.

Second, it can help to reduce the amount of stress and anxiety you experience when interacting with a narcissist or toxic person.

Third, it can help to de-escalate tense situations and prevent them from becoming explosive.

How to Grey Rock

1. Limit Your Interactions: One of the best ways to use the grey rocking technique is to limit your interactions with the narcissist or toxic person as much as possible. This might mean avoiding them altogether or only interacting with them when absolutely necessary.

2. Keep It Short and Sweet: When you need to interact with a narcissist or toxic person, keep your responses short and to the point. Avoid engaging in small talk or providing any personal information that they could use against you.

3. Be Boring: When communicating with the narcissist or toxic person, aim to be as boring and uninteresting as possible. Avoid showing any emotion or enthusiasm and keep your tone

neutral and uninvolved.

4. Don't Argue: One of the key tactics of a narcissist or toxic person is to provoke others into an argument. Don't take the bait. Instead, calmly state your opinion and then disengage from the conversation.

5. Avoid Reacting: When the narcissist or toxic person tries to provoke you, avoid reacting emotionally. Instead, remain calm and composed, and respond with neutral statements like "okay" or "I see."

6. Use neutral body language and tone: When communicating with the toxic person, use neutral body language and tone to convey your lack of interest or engagement. Avoid making eye contact for extended periods, keep your voice calm and even, and try not to show any strong emotional reactions.

7. Don't give the toxic person any emotional ammunition: One of the key aspects of grey rocking is not giving the toxic person any emotional ammunition to use against you. This means avoiding sharing personal information or opinions that the person could use to manipulate or control you later on. Stick to neutral topics and avoid sharing any information that could be used against you in the future.

8. Disengage as quickly as possible: If the toxic person becomes aggressive or hostile, it's important to disengage as quickly as possible. This may mean getting up and leaving the room, breaking off the conversation, or simply ignoring the person's behavior and continuing on with your day as usual.

9. Set Boundaries: It's important to set clear boundaries with the narcissist or toxic person. Let them know what behaviors

are not acceptable and what consequences they will face if they violate these boundaries.

I used this technique very effectively with my personality-disorder-diagnosed ex-husband. Not only did it protect me from his constant abuse, but it also protected our children to an extent. He would do things that upset them to get a reaction out of me. When I stopped reacting, his abuse lessened.

Grey rocking also helped me in our court battles.

Divorcing a personality-disordered person is the most difficult thing I have ever been through. The injustice of his accusations was infuriating. He would use my justified reaction to his behavior to say that I was unbalanced to our children's therapist and court personnel. When I stopped reacting and grey-rocked him, it gave me back my power and showed the people in charge of our case who was actually causing the problems with the children.

Grey Rocking can work with anyone who crosses your boundaries to get a reaction, including spouses, parents, your boss, or people in your community.

Dealing with a narcissist or toxic person can be incredibly challenging, but using the grey rocking technique can help to make these interactions more manageable. By limiting your interactions, keeping your responses short and to the point, being boring, avoiding arguments, not reacting emotionally, and setting clear boundaries, you can reduce the amount of emotional fuel you provide and starve the narcissist or toxic person of the attention they crave.

Remember, grey rocking is not about being passive or submissive; it's about taking control of the situation and protecting your emotional well-being.

A Meditation for Healing from a Relationship with a Narcissist

Before you begin, find a quiet place where you won't be interrupted. Sit or lie down in a comfortable position, and take a few deep breaths to calm your mind and body.

Visualize yourself in a safe and peaceful place. This could be a beach, a forest, or any place where you feel calm and relaxed.

Take a moment to observe your surroundings and notice the sights, sounds, and smells.

Breathe deeply and inhale the fresh air around you.

Feel the sun on your skin or the cool breeze on your face.

Now, visualize the person who hurt you.

Imagine them standing in front of you, and allow any negative emotions to rise to the surface.

Let yourself feel the anger, hurt, and sadness that you may hold on to. Acknowledge these emotions and allow yourself to feel them fully.

As you continue to breathe deeply and let go of negative emotions, visualize them leaving your body.

Imagine each negative emotion as a dark cloud that is slowly drifting away from you, leaving you feeling lighter and more peaceful.

Now, imagine a rope in front of you.

This represents the connection you had with the narcissist.

Grab onto the rope and feel the weight of it.

Acknowledge the pain that the relationship caused you, but also remember that it is in the past.

It's time to let go of this rope and release the connection to the narcissist.

Take a deep breath and let go of the rope.

Watch it drift away from you, disappearing into the distance.

As the rope disappears, allow yourself to feel a sense of release and freedom.

You are no longer connected to the narcissist and are free to move forward with your life.

Visualize yourself surrounded by a warm, healing light.

This light represents the love and support that is available to you.

Allow this light to penetrate every cell in your body, bringing healing and peace.

As you bask in this healing light, repeat the following affirmations to yourself:

I release the pain and hurt from my past relationship.

I am worthy of love and respect.

I am free to move forward and create a fulfilling life for myself.

Take a few deep breaths and allow yourself to fully embrace these affirmations.

When you're ready, slowly open your eyes and return to your surroundings.

TOXIC RELATIONSHIPS

If you attempt to set boundaries with someone and they continually cross them, you are probably dealing with a toxic person. A relationship with a toxic person can have a detrimental impact on your life. These relationships can lead to mental health problems, such as anxiety, depression, and low self-esteem. They can negatively affect your physical health, and cause issues such as headaches, fatigue, chronic stress, chronic pain, or autoimmune diseases, and can also affect your work performance and social life.

You deserve to be treated with respect and kindness, and it's okay to prioritize your well-being over toxic relationships. Identifying toxic people can be challenging, but it's essential to protect yourself from their harmful behavior. Pay attention to how they make you feel and how they behave towards others. Trust your instincts and don't ignore red flags. It's always better to distance yourself from toxic people than to suffer the consequences of their actions.

It is not always easy to identify a toxic relationship, as these relationships can take on different forms. A toxic relationship can be with a friend, family member, partner, or colleague.

However, some common signs of a toxic relationship are:

Constant criticism

Manipulation and control

Lack of trust and respect

Emotional or physical abuse

Feeling drained or exhausted after spending time with the person

Crossing boundaries repeatedly

Feeling like you are always walking on eggshells around them

These are some examples of toxic relationships.

1. The Caretaker and the Dependent - In this type of relationship, one person takes on the role of the caretaker, while the other becomes the dependent.

The caretaker feels responsible for the dependent's well-being and often sacrifices their own needs to cater to the dependent's needs. The dependent, on the other hand, become reliant on the caretaker, and their self-esteem and sense of worth become tied to the caretaker's care.

This relationship can quickly become toxic as the caretaker may begin to feel burdened and resentful of the dependent's constant need for attention and care. The dependent may also feel trapped in the relationship and unable to take responsibility for their own life, leading to a cycle of dependency.

There are healthy relationships that involve caregiving, but both members of the relationship must feel cared for and that the burden of caregiving is not one-sided.

2. The Fixer and the Victim - In this type of relationship, one person takes on the role of the fixer, while the other becomes the victim.

The fixer feels responsible for the victim's problems and often tries to solve them or make them go away. The victim becomes reliant on the fixer and may even unconsciously create problems to keep the fixer around.

This relationship can quickly become toxic, as the fixer may feel overwhelmed and frustrated by the victim's constant problems. The victim may also feel powerless and unable to take responsibility for their own life, leading to a cycle of victimhood.

3. The Martyr and the Guilt-Tripper - In this type of relationship, one person takes on the role of the martyr, while the other becomes the guilt-tripper.

The martyr feels responsible for the guilt-tripper's emotions and often sacrifices their own happiness to avoid triggering negative emotions in the guilt-tripper. The guilt-tripper may use guilt as a tool to manipulate the martyr into doing what they want.

This relationship can quickly become toxic as the martyr may feel trapped and resentful of the guilt-tripper's emotional manipulation. The guilt-tripper may also feel entitled to the martyr's sacrifice, leading to a cycle of emotional abuse.

It's important to remember that you have the power to leave a toxic relationship if it's not serving you. This can be a difficult decision, but it's important to prioritize your well-being and safety above all else.

You might benefit from seeking the help of a therapist, who can help you navigate these relationships and develop healthy coping mechanisms. If you're feeling unsafe or unhappy in a relationship, it's important to seek help and support in leaving it.

Dealing with toxic relationships can be incredibly stressful, but it's important to remember that you're not alone. Remember that you deserve to be treated with respect and kindness and that you have the power to create a life that supports your well-being.

A Meditation for Healing from a Toxic Relationship

Close your eyes and take a deep breath in through your nose, filling your lungs with air. Hold the breath for a few seconds, then release it slowly through your mouth. Do this a few times, allowing yourself to relax and let go of any tension in your body.

As you continue to breathe deeply, focus your attention on your breath. Notice the sensation of the air moving in and out of your nostrils, the rise and fall of your chest, and the movement of your belly. Try to keep your mind from wandering by gently guiding it back to your breath whenever you notice it has drifted away.

Visualize a bright light shining on you, starting at the top of your head and slowly moving down your body.

As the light moves down, it fills you with healing energy. This energy is cleansing and purifying, removing any negative emotions or thoughts that may hold you back.

As the light continues to move down your body, it reaches your heart center. Visualize the light entering your heart and filling it with love and compassion.

Imagine this love and compassion spreading out from your heart and enveloping your entire being. As you continue to focus on your heart center, think about any pain or hurt that you may still carry from your toxic relationship.

Recognize these emotions and allow yourself to feel them fully.

Acknowledge that these emotions are a part of your healing process, but that they do not define you.

As you continue to breathe deeply, imagine sending love and compassion to yourself. Visualize wrapping yourself in a warm blanket of love and kindness. Allow yourself to feel the warmth and comfort of this love.

Visualize the warm, healing light that surrounds you.

Imagine this light as a protective shield that can help you let go of any negative emotions or thoughts that may hold you back.

Allow this light to penetrate your body, filling you with peace and tranquility.

Repeat the following affirmations to yourself, either silently or out loud:

"I am worthy of love and respect."

"I am strong and capable."

"I deserve to be happy and fulfilled."

Allow yourself to feel these affirmations deeply as if they are already true. Remember that you are not defined by your past experiences and that you have the power to create a better future for yourself.

As you continue to meditate, allow yourself to release any negative emotions that may hold you back. If you feel anger, sadness, or fear, acknowledge these emotions without judgment. Allow them to pass through you like waves, without holding onto them or trying to push them away.

Take a moment to think about all the things that you are thankful for in your life. Think about the people who love and support you, the experiences that have brought you joy, and the opportunities that await you.

Allow yourself to feel a sense of gratitude and appreciation for all the blessings in your life.

When you are ready to end your meditation, take a deep breath in and slowly release it through your mouth.

Narcissitic Parents and Boundaries

Narcissistic parents are those who are primarily concerned with their own needs and desires, often at the expense of their children's well-being. Growing up with a narcissistic parent can be a grueling experience. As a result, children of narcissistic parents often grow up feeling unheard, unimportant, and unloved.

Unfortunately, these experiences can have lasting effects on your relationships as adults, particularly when it comes to your ability to have your needs met and setting and enforcing healthy boundaries. Having a narcissistic parent can set us up for having co-dependent and toxic relationships as adults.

Children of narcissists often develop a strong sense of self-reliance and independence, as they learn early on that they cannot rely on their parents for emotional support or validation. This sense of self-reliance can also lead to an unhealthy pattern of seeking partners who also do not meet their emotional needs. This can manifest in a variety of ways, such as choosing partners who are emotionally distant, ignoring red flags in relationships, or staying in relationships that are not fulfilling.

If your parent is a narcissist, you may have learned unhealthy relationship patterns that carry over into your adult life.

Children of narcissistic parents often learn to suppress their own needs and desires in order to avoid conflict or attention from their parents. This can lead to a lack of self-awareness, as we may not even know what our own needs are. As a result, we may enter into relationships where we don't even know what we want, much less how to communicate those wants to our partner.

Even if we know what our needs are, we may be afraid to ask for them. Growing up with a narcissistic parent can teach us that expressing our needs is dangerous, as it can lead to criticism, rejection, or even punishment. As a result, we may enter into relationships where we don't ask for what we need and instead hope our partner will "know" what we want.

Narcissistic parents are often emotionally unavailable themselves, which can lead their children to seek similar partners in adulthood. We may be attracted to people who are emotionally distant or unresponsive because that feels familiar to us. Unfortunately, this can lead to relationships where our needs for emotional connection and intimacy are not being met.

Children of narcissistic parents often learn to be accommodating and people-pleasing in order to avoid conflict. As adults, we may continue this pattern by being overly accommodating in our relationships, putting our own needs aside in order to make our partners happy, and taking responsibility for things that are not our responsibility. While compromise is important in any relationship, being overly accommodating, and taking on too much, can lead to a lack of balance and a feeling of resentment over time.

Narcissistic parents often have poor boundaries themselves and may not respect their children's boundaries either. As a result, children of narcissistic parents may not learn how to set and maintain healthy boundaries in their own relationships. We may be afraid to say "no" to our partner, or may not even know how to establish boundaries in the first place.

One of the most significant impacts of being raised by a narcissistic parent is a lack of trust in our own emotions and instincts. Children of narcissistic parents are often told that their feelings are wrong or invalid and may grow up doubting their own emotions. This can lead to difficulty in recognizing our own needs and desires, and can make it challenging to communicate those needs to our partners.

Having a parent who is a narcissist or has a toxic personality can be extremely challenging. It's difficult to navigate a relationship with someone who only sees things from their own perspective and is often selfish and manipulative in their behavior.

However, it is possible to have a relationship with a narcissistic or toxic parent if you know how to deal with them effectively. Grey rocking your parent can help you maintain a relationship with a difficult parent while protecting your own emotional well-being.

It's important to be aware of your own emotions when dealing with a narcissistic or toxic parent. Try to remain calm and don't let their behavior affect you too much. Remember that their behavior is not a reflection of your worth as a person.

Keep conversations short and to the point. When talking to a narcissistic or toxic parent, keep your conversations brief and focused. Don't engage in long discussions or arguments, as this will only give them more fuel.

Avoid giving your parent emotional reactions. Narcissistic and toxic people thrive on drama and emotional reactions, so it's important to avoid giving them the satisfaction of seeing you upset or angry. Try to remain neutral and unemotional in your interactions with them.

Narcissistic and toxic people often use personal information to manipulate and control others. Avoid sharing personal details about your life with narcissistic parents, as this will only give them more ammunition to use against you.

It's important to set clear boundaries with a narcissistic or toxic parent. Let them know what behavior is acceptable and what is not, and stick to your boundaries even when they try to push your limits.

Narcissistic and toxic parents often use emotional manipulation to get what they want. They may try to provoke you or elicit a strong emotional response in order to feel powerful and in control. If your parent does this, try not to take the bait. Stay calm and neutral, and don't give them the satisfaction of seeing you upset or angry.

Narcissistic and toxic parents often thrive on power struggles and control. Don't engage in power struggles with your parent, as this will only give them more power over you. Instead, focus on maintaining your own sense of control and independence.

By remaining emotionally neutral and uninteresting to them, you can deprive them of the attention and drama they crave, making them lose interest in you and eventually leave you alone. With these strategies, you can maintain a relationship with a narcissistic or toxic parent while protecting your own emotional well-being.

Breaking the cycle of seeking relationships where our needs are not being met can be a long and difficult process. It requires us to confront painful memories from our childhood and learn how to express our own needs and emotions. But with the help of therapy and a supportive community, it is possible to break free from the cycle and build healthy relationships.

If you identify with any of the patterns listed above, consider seeking therapy or counseling to help you work through those issues. A trained therapist can help you gain self-awareness, learn healthy communication and boundary-setting skills, and develop more fulfilling relationships.

Remember, you deserve to have your needs met in your relationships and with the right support, you can learn how to make that happen.

A Meditation for Healing from a Narcissistic Parent

Take a deep breath in, and as you exhale, let go of any tension in your body.

Take another deep breath in, and as you exhale, visualize a bright light surrounding you, protecting you, and filling you with love and warmth.

Now, bring to mind the image of your narcissistic parent.

As you do so, notice any emotions or physical sensations that arise.

Allow yourself to feel whatever comes up, without judgment or resistance. Simply observe these feelings and sensations with compassion and gentleness.

As you continue to focus on the image of your narcissistic parent, visualize a bubble forming around them.

This bubble represents their energy field, and it's separate from yours.

Notice any feelings of relief or safety that come from creating this boundary.

Now, imagine a beam of white light coming down from above, and shining directly onto your narcissistic parent.

This light represents healing and love, and it's meant to help them heal from their own wounds and challenges.

Visualize this light washing over them, filling them with a sense of peace and love.

As you continue to focus on this image, notice any emotions or physical sensations that arise within you.

Allow yourself to feel whatever comes up, without judgment or resistance.

Simply observe these feelings and sensations with compassion and gentleness.

Now, bring to mind the image of yourself as a child, and visualize yourself standing in front of your narcissistic parent.

As you look at your younger self, notice any emotions or physical sensations that arise.

Allow yourself to feel whatever comes up, without judgment or resistance. Simply observe these feelings and sensations with compassion and gentleness.

As you continue to focus on the image of yourself as a child, imagine a beam of golden light coming down from above and shining directly onto you.

This light represents healing and love, and it's meant to help you heal from your own wounds and challenges.

Visualize this light washing over you, filling you with a sense of peace and love.

As you continue to focus on this image, notice any emotions or physical sensations that arise within you.

Allow yourself to feel whatever comes up, without judgment or resistance.

Simply observe these feelings and sensations with compassion and gentleness.

Now, visualize the bubble around your narcissistic parent beginning to shrink and disappear.

As it does so, notice any emotions or physical sensations that arise. Allow yourself to feel whatever comes up, without judgment or resistance. Simply observe these feelings and sensations with compassion and gentleness.

Now, imagine that you are sitting in a beautiful garden. The sun is shining, and you can hear the birds singing. You feel safe and at peace.

As you look around the garden, you notice a path that leads to a small pond.

You decide to walk towards it.

As you approach the pond, you notice your reflection in the water.

Take a moment to look at yourself. Observe your physical appearance, your emotions, and your thoughts. Notice any feelings that come up, but do not judge them. Just observe them and let them be.

Now, imagine that your narcissistic parent appears next to you.

They may look angry, critical, or dismissive.

Notice how you feel in their presence. Take a deep breath and remind yourself that you are safe and protected in this garden. That your parent is in the bubble which protects you.

You have the power to control your emotions and reactions.

As you look at your parent, repeat the following affirmations silently to yourself:

I am worthy of love and respect.

My parent's behavior is not a reflection of my worth.

I choose to release the pain and hurt of the past.

I forgive myself for any mistakes I made in the past.

I choose to let go of any negative beliefs about myself.

I am capable of creating a happy and fulfilling life for myself.

Take a few deep breaths and feel the weight of these affirmations in your heart.

Feel the love and compassion that you have for yourself. You are a strong, resilient, and beautiful person who deserves happiness and fulfillment.

Now, imagine that your parent is leaving.

As they walk away, feel a sense of relief and freedom. You no longer need to carry the burden of their emotional baggage. You are free to live your life on your terms with no guilt or shame.

Finally, bring to mind the image of yourself in the present moment, surrounded by the bright light you visualized at the beginning of this meditation.

Notice any emotions or physical sensations that arise within you.

Allow yourself to feel whatever comes up, without judgment or resistance. Simply observe these feelings and sensations with compassion and gentleness.

Take a deep breath in, and as you exhale, visualize the bright light surrounding you beginning to shrink and disappear. As it does so, notice any emotions or physical sensations that arise.

Allow yourself to feel whatever comes up, without judgment or resistance.

Simply observe these feelings and sensations with compassion and gentleness.

When you're ready, slowly open your eyes and take a few deep breaths.

Notice how you feel, and allow yourself to sit with any emotions or physical sensations that arise.

BOUNDARY SETTING WITH TOXIC PEOPLE

S etting boundaries with toxic people is one of the most challenging things to do in life. Whether it's your family members, friends, or colleagues, toxic people have a way of making you feel responsible for their behavior. They may use manipulation, guilt-tripping, sulking, or even threats to make you feel like you have to let them cross your boundaries.

Unfortunately, if we don't learn to set healthy boundaries with toxic individuals, it can seriously harm our mental, emotional, and physical well-being.

When we set healthy boundaries, we are essentially saying "no" to things that do not serve us or align with our values, and "yes" to things that do. This can include saying no to toxic behavior, negative energy, and disrespect, and saying yes to self-care, positivity, and healthy relationships. It's important to protect our mental, emotional, and physical health from people who drain us of our energy and happiness. It's important to remember that it's not your job to fix or care for everyone and that it's okay to prioritize your own needs and well-being.

Whether it's a romantic partner, a friend, or a family member, dealing with someone who is constantly negative, critical, or emotionally draining can take a significant toll on your mental and emotional well-being. What exactly is the person doing that is causing harm to you? It could be anything from verbal abuse, to emotional manipulation, or physical aggression. Make a list of the toxic behavior, so you have a clear understanding of what you're dealing with.

You are not powerless in these situations. By setting healthy boundaries and focusing on stress management techniques, you can take control of your own mental health and reduce the impact of toxic relationships on your life.

One of the reasons why we can struggle with setting boundaries is due to a lack of self-worth. We may feel that we don't deserve to be treated with respect and kindness, and as a result, we allow others to treat us poorly. It is crucial to understand that you are worthy of love and respect, and it is your right to set boundaries to protect yourself.

It's important to set healthy boundaries in any relationship, but it is critical to set boundaries in a toxic relationship. Boundaries can help protect your mental and emotional health and give you a sense of control in a situation that may feel overwhelming. This means being clear about what you will and won't tolerate, and communicating those boundaries to the other person.

Healthy boundaries can include anything from limiting contact with the person to setting clear expectations for how you will interact with them. Maybe you only communicate by email so you have a record of conversations, or you limit the length or frequency of visits.

Setting boundaries can be difficult, especially if you're used to being a people-pleaser or if the other person is used to getting their way. But it's important to remember that setting boundaries is not selfish, it's a necessary step in protecting your mental health.

For example, if your boss is constantly criticizing you, you might say something like, "I appreciate your feedback, but I would prefer if we could focus on constructive criticism."

If your partner is emotionally manipulating you, you might say something like, "I feel uncomfortable when you try to guilt-trip me. Can we find a healthier way to communicate?" If they continue to manipulate you, tell them the consequences if they continue to do it, and then follow through with what you told them you would do if they continued to cross your boundary.

If a friend is always talking about their problems without ever asking about yours, you might let them know that you need more balance in your conversations.

It is important to communicate your boundaries with the person who has been crossing them. This can be a difficult conversation to have, but it's important to be clear and assertive. Clearly and specifically state what behavior is acceptable and what is not.

The toxic person may try to test your boundaries or push back against them. It's important to stay firm and consistent in enforcing your boundaries. This may mean limiting or ending contact with the person if they continue to cross your boundaries.

It is essential to communicate your boundaries in a calm and assertive manner. Avoid being confrontational or aggressive, as this can escalate the situation. Let the person know what behaviors are unacceptable and what the consequences will be if they continue to cross your boundaries. It's important to follow through with the consequences if the person continues to violate your boundaries.

If you feel nervous about communicating your boundaries with someone, the support of a therapist can help you and also give you a safe space in which to have these conversations.

It is easy to fall back into old patterns of behavior, but it is crucial to remain consistent. If someone crosses your boundaries, remind them of your boundaries and the consequences of crossing them. If they continue to cross your boundaries, it may be time to reevaluate the relationship.

Dealing with toxic people can be stressful and emotionally draining. It's important to seek support from friends, family, or a therapist. Talking to someone who understands what you're going through can help you process your emotions and come up with strategies for dealing with the toxic person.

Changing our ingrained patterns of behavior can be challenging, but with time and practice, we can learn to set healthy boundaries and protect ourselves from toxic people. While it may be challenging to change our ingrained patterns of behavior, it's worth it, in the long run, to prioritize our own needs and establish healthy relationships with those around us.

A MEDITATION TO STOP ENABLING OTHERS BEHAVIORS

Close your eyes and take a few deep breaths to relax your body and mind.

Now, focus your attention on your breath.

Notice the sensation of the air flowing in and out of your nostrils and the rise and fall of your chest.

As you continue to breathe, allow your thoughts to come and go without getting attached to them. If you notice your mind wandering, gently bring your attention back to your breath.

Now, bring to mind a person in your life whose behavior you enable. It could be a friend, family member, or partner. Visualize them in your mind and observe how you feel when you think about them.

As you focus on this person, ask yourself the following questions:

How does their behavior affect me?

Why do I enable their behavior?

What are the consequences of enabling their behavior?

Allow yourself to explore these questions without judgment or criticism. Be honest with yourself and acknowledge what you are feeling.

It's okay to feel uncomfortable or uneasy. Remember that this is a part of the process of self-discovery and growth.

As you breathe in, say to yourself, "I am aware of my enabling behavior." As you breathe out, say, "I choose to stop enabling others."

Repeat this affirmation with each breath, allowing yourself to fully embrace the intention to stop enabling others.

Now, visualize yourself setting boundaries with this person.

Imagine yourself calmly and assertively communicating your needs and expectations.

See yourself standing up for yourself and not tolerating their unacceptable behavior.

Visualize yourself taking care of your own needs and well-being, without sacrificing them for someone else.

As you visualize this scenario, notice how you feel. Do you feel empowered, confident, and in control?

Allow yourself to experience these emotions fully.

Know that you have the power to stop enabling others' behaviors and create healthy and fulfilling relationships.

When you are ready, take a few deep breaths and slowly open your eyes.

Take a moment to reflect on your meditation and the insights you gained.

BOUNDARY SETTING AT WORK

As employees, we all want to be seen as team players and show our commitment to our job. However, there may be times when a boss asks us to take on tasks outside the scope of our duties or to work when we are off the clock. While it may be tempting to say yes, it's important to set boundaries in order to protect both our personal and professional lives. While it's important to be flexible and adaptable in the workplace, it's also crucial to set boundaries to ensure that we are not overworked or taken advantage of.

Setting boundaries is not a negative thing. It's not a sign of laziness or lack of commitment to your job. Rather, it's a sign of self-respect and a commitment to maintaining a healthy work-life balance. When we set boundaries, we are showing our bosses and colleagues that we value our time and energy, and that we want to ensure we are giving our best to every task we take on.

One of the most important things you can do is to know your job description inside and out. This will help you identify when your boss is asking you to do something outside of your duties. If you're unsure about what your job description entails, don't be afraid to ask for clarification from your boss or HR.

If your boss is continually asking you to do things outside of your job description or crossing boundaries, it's important to document your concerns. This will help you keep track of the issue and provide evidence if needed. Write down specific instances where your boss has asked you to do something outside of your job description or crossed a boundary that you have set. Keep a record of emails, conversations, and any other relevant information that can support your case. This will help you if you need to escalate the situation to HR or seek legal advice.

Once you have a clear understanding of your job description and have documented your concerns, it's time to talk to your boss. Schedule a meeting with your boss, and bring your documentation with you. Be clear and specific about your concerns and provide examples of when your boss has crossed a boundary or asked you to do something outside of your job description. Remember to remain professional and respectful during the conversation.

If you are being asked to work outside of your regular working hours, it's important to communicate your availability. Let your boss know your work hours and the times you are not available. If it's an urgent matter, ask if it can wait until you are back in the office or if there is someone else who can handle it. Let your boss know that you are happy to help out, but that you have other responsibilities and commitments that you need to attend to outside of work hours.

If you're unable to take on a task or work outside of your normal hours, try to offer alternatives. For example, you may be able to delegate the task to another colleague or suggest a different timeline that works better for you.

It's important to be assertive when setting boundaries, but it's equally important to be respectful. Remember to be polite and professional when communicating your boundaries to your boss. It's also helpful to provide a reason for why you cannot take on the task at that time.

If your boss is asking you to take on a task that you cannot complete at that time, offer a solution. Let your boss know when you can complete the task or suggest someone else who may be able to help. Offering solutions shows that you are committed to finding a resolution.

Once you have set your boundaries, it's important to stick to them. Don't let your boss or colleagues pressure you into taking on tasks or working outside of your regular hours. Remember that your time and well-being are important and should be respected.

If your boss is continually asking you to do things outside of your job description or crossing boundaries, seek support from trusted colleagues and mentors. Talking to someone who has been in a similar situation can help you gain perspective and come up with a plan of action.

If you have tried everything in your power to address the situation and your boss is still crossing boundaries or asking you to do things outside of your job description, it may be time to escalate the issue. Contact Human Resources and explain the situation, providing any documentation you have. HR will investigate the matter and take appropriate action to protect your rights as an employee.

If you can't get the support you need, it may be time to polish your resume, and start looking for a new job with a company that will respect you.

THE POWER OF SAYING NO: A MEDITATION

Find a quiet place where you can sit comfortably for a few minutes. Close your eyes and take a deep breath in, exhaling slowly.

As you continue to breathe deeply, bring to mind a situation where you struggled to say no.

Perhaps it was a work project you didn't have time for, a social event you didn't want to attend, or a request for help that you didn't have the energy for. Whatever it was, allow yourself to feel the emotions that come up without judgment.

Notice any physical sensations in your body, such as tightness in your chest or a knot in your stomach.

Now, imagine yourself standing in front of a mirror.

Look deeply into your own eyes and say out loud, "I have the power to say no."

Repeat this several times until you feel a sense of empowerment.

Next, visualize a bubble of white light surrounding you. This bubble represents your personal boundaries.

As you breathe in, imagine the bubble growing larger and more solid.

As you exhale, imagine any stress or negativity that may try to penetrate your boundaries being released from your body and mind.

Now, bring to mind the situation you were struggling with earlier.

Imagine yourself standing in front of the person who made the request.

Take a deep breath and say, "I'm sorry, but I won't be able to help with this."

Notice how you feel in your body and mind as you say these words.

Do you feel a sense of relief or tension?

Acknowledge these feelings without judging them.

As you say "no," notice how it feels in your body. Do you feel relieved or guilty? Allow yourself to experience these emotions without judgment.

Take a few more deep breaths, inhaling and exhaling slowly.

As you continue to observe your breath, bring to mind a situation where you said yes when you really wanted to say no.

Perhaps it was agreeing to take on extra work at the office or attending an event that you didn't really want to go to.

Allow yourself to feel the discomfort of that situation. Now, bring to mind a situation where you said no and felt empowered by your decision.

Perhaps it was turning down a job offer that didn't align with your values or declining an invitation to an event that didn't interest you.

Allow yourself to feel the sense of relief and empowerment that came from saying no.

As you continue to focus on your breath, repeat the following affirmations to yourself:

Saying no is a powerful act of self-care.

I am allowed to prioritize my own needs and desires.

Saying no to others is saying yes to myself.

Visualize yourself confidently saying no to a situation that doesn't serve you. See yourself standing tall and feeling strong in your decision. Imagine the positive impact that saying no has on your life and the lives of those around you.

When you are ready, slowly open your eyes and return to the present moment.

By practicing this meditation regularly, you can strengthen your ability to say "no" when it is necessary. Remember that setting boundaries and prioritizing your own needs is not selfish, it is a necessary part of self-care and well-being. With time and practice, you can tap into the power of saying "no" and create a more balanced and fulfilling life.

LIVING YOUR LIFE IN A SUPPORTING ROLE

When we feel responsible for caring for and supporting others, it can prevent us from pursuing our own dreams. We have been taught to put the needs of others before our own. We may have grown up in families where self-sacrifice was valued, or we may have been conditioned by society to believe that putting others first is the right thing to do. We may not even realize that we are sacrificing our dreams, goals, and ambitions in service of others.

While it's certainly admirable to be selfless and supportive, it's important to remember that we also have our own goals and dreams and that they are just as important as those of the people in our lives. It is okay to prioritize ourselves and take the time to do things that make us happy and fulfilled.

When we choose to act in a supporting role, we are essentially putting our own dreams on hold to help others achieve theirs. This may involve sacrificing our time, energy, and resources to ensure that others are successful. While there is nothing wrong with helping others, it is important to remember that we should not neglect our own dreams and aspirations.

We are not being selfish when we pursue our passions.

As human beings, we are naturally inclined to support and help those around us. Whether it's a friend, family member, or colleague, we often find ourselves in situations where we need to lend a hand. But when we put our own dreams on hold in order to support others, we run the risk of living a life of regret and dissatisfaction. It's easy to fall into the trap of thinking that we'll have plenty of time to pursue our own goals later in life, but time is finite. We only have so many years on this earth, and it's up to us to make the most of them.

That's not to say that we should abandon our loved ones or neglect our responsibilities in order to pursue our own dreams. Rather, it's about finding a way to support others while also making space for our own aspirations. This might mean setting aside time each week to work on our own projects, or it might mean finding a job or role that allows us to use our skills and talents while still supporting others.

One way to strike this balance is to communicate openly with the people in our lives. Let your partners, friends, and family members know that you have your own goals and passions and that you want to find a way to pursue them while still supporting them.

This might mean compromising on certain things, or it might mean finding creative solutions that work for everyone.

We need to recognize our own value and contributions. We need to be confident in our abilities and recognize that we deserve credit for our hard work and ideas. This doesn't mean being arrogant or boastful, but rather having a healthy sense of self-worth and confidence.

We need to be assertive in advocating for ourselves. This can be difficult, particularly if we're used to being more behind-the-scenes or accommodating to others. But it's important to speak up and assert our own contributions when necessary. This doesn't mean being confrontational or aggressive, but rather being clear and direct in communicating our value.

We can't always say yes to every request or opportunity that comes our way, especially if it comes at the expense of our own growth and development. We need to be strategic in how we support others, making sure that we're also advocating for ourselves and our own goals.

We can't always let others take credit for our work or ideas, as this diminishes our own accomplishments and potential. Acting in a supporting role is a noble and important thing to do, but it should not come at the expense of your own dreams and aspirations.

It is essential to find a balance between supporting others and pursuing our own passions. By prioritizing ourselves and communicating our needs, we can avoid feelings of regret and resentment and live a more fulfilling life. By being confident, assertive, and mindful of our own priorities, we can strike a balance between supporting others and advocating for ourselves.

A MEDITATION: I CAN BE THE STAR OF MY OWN LIFE

C lose your eyes and take a deep breath in, filling your lungs completely.

Hold your breath for a moment, then exhale slowly, letting go of any tension in your body.

Take a few more deep breaths like this, focusing on the sensation of the air moving in and out of your body.

Feel your chest rise and fall with each inhale and exhale.

As you breathe, imagine that you are breathing in a bright,

white light that fills your body with energy and vitality.

With each exhale, imagine that you are releasing any negative thoughts or emotions that may be holding you back.

Now, imagine that you are standing on a stage, surrounded by darkness.

You are the only one there, but you feel empowered and confident.

The spotlight is on you, and you are the star of the show. You feel a sense of excitement and anticipation, knowing that you are about to embark on a journey of self-discovery and empowerment.

As you stand there, take a moment to reflect on your life.

Think about all the things you have accomplished and the challenges you have overcome.

Remember all the times you have felt afraid or unsure, and how you pushed through those moments to come out stronger.

Now, imagine that you are holding a microphone in your hand. This microphone represents your voice and your power.

You have the power to speak up, to make choices, and to change your life. You are in control of your own destiny, and you have the ability to make your dreams a reality.

Take a deep breath and say to yourself, "I am the star of my own life. I have the power to create my own happiness and success."

Repeat this affirmation to yourself as many times as you need to until you truly believe it.

As you continue to hold the microphone, think about what you want to say to the world. What message do you want to share? What words of inspiration or wisdom do you want to offer?

Take a moment to reflect on your purpose and your passion, and then speak your truth into the microphone.

Feel the power of your words as they resonate through the stage and out into the world.

Imagine the impact that you can have on others by sharing your message and your voice.

You know you are the star of your own life, and that you have the power to create the life you want.

As you stand there, imagine that a spotlight suddenly shines down on you. It illuminates your entire body, and you feel yourself glowing with radiant energy.

You feel proud of who you are and all that you have accomplished.

You know you are capable of achieving anything you set your mind to.

As you bask in the spotlight, take a moment to reflect on your life.

Think about the things that make you happy, the things that inspire you, and the things that you want to achieve.

Imagine that each of these things is a star in the sky, twinkling brightly.

Now, imagine that you are reaching up to the sky and plucking these stars out of the sky, one by one.

Each star represents a different aspect of your life, whether it's your career, your relationships, your hobbies, or your personal growth.

Hold each star in your hand and examine it closely. Think about what it represents and what you want to achieve in this area of your life. As you hold each star, feel yourself becoming more and more empowered.

You know that you have the power to shape your own destiny and that you can make your dreams a reality.

With each star you hold, feel your confidence growing stronger.

When you have examined each star, place them back in the sky and imagine that they are shining even brighter than before.

You know you will achieve your goals and fulfill your dreams because you are the star of your own life.

Take a few deep breaths, then slowly open your eyes.

Take a moment to reflect on the meditation and how it made you feel.

DEALING WITH GUILT

There comes a time when we must prioritize ourselves and stop taking on responsibilities that are not ours to bear. Those we are close to can become dependent on us doing things, and when we stop, we may feel guilty.

We all experience guilt at some point in our lives. Guilt is a feeling of remorse or regret for something we have done or failed to do. It is a powerful emotion that can weigh heavily on our minds and hearts.

Guilt is a normal and healthy emotion that we all experience from time to time. It can serve as a signal that we have done something wrong or violated our own values or beliefs.

However, not all guilt is created equal. There are two types of guilt: healthy guilt and unhealthy guilt.

Healthy guilt is a productive emotion that motivates us to take responsibility for our actions and make amends when necessary. Healthy guilt is an appropriate response to doing something wrong, such as hurting someone's feelings, breaking a promise, or not living up to our own standards. It prompts us to make amends and take responsibility for our actions. If you have hurt others, it is important to make amends. Apologize and take responsibility for your actions. This can help you move past your guilt and restore your relationships.

Healthy guilt helps us to learn from our mistakes and to make positive changes in our lives. It is a natural consequence of violating our own values or hurting others. Healthy guilt helps us grow as individuals.

Unhealthy guilt is a paralyzing emotion that can be debilitating. It results from unrealistic expectations, self-doubt, and negative self-talk.

Unhealthy guilt can make us feel like we are not doing enough, even when we are doing everything we can. It can also lead to feelings of anxiety, depression, and low self-esteem. Unhealthy guilt is an irrational and excessive feeling of guilt that is not based on real wrongdoing. External pressures or unrealistic expectations that we place on ourselves often cause unhealthy guilt. Unhealthy guilt can lead to feelings of self-doubt, anxiety, and even depression.

It is normal to feel guilty when you stop doing things for others, but it is important to recognize that your own needs are just as important.

It is important to handle the situation in the best possible way so that we don't feel guilty about stopping it. Here are some steps that you can take when you decide you can't do something for someone you have been doing:

Evaluate the situation and understand why you can't continue doing it. Is it because you don't have the time or resources? Is it because it is affecting your mental or physical health? Once you have a clear understanding of the situation, you can move forward.

Communicate your decision clearly to the person you have been helping. Be honest and transparent about why you can't continue doing it. Don't beat around the bush or make excuses. It is important to calmly and clearly communicate your decision to stop doing things for others. Put yourself in the other person's shoes and understand how they might feel. Acknowledge their feelings and apologize for any inconvenience caused. Showing empathy will make the other person more understanding of your decision. Let them know you are not doing it to hurt them but to take care of yourself. This will help to ease their concerns and reduce any guilt they may be feeling.

Just because you can't continue doing something doesn't mean that you can't help in other ways. Offer alternatives to the person you have been helping. Maybe you can help them find someone else who can help them. Or maybe you can offer to help in a different way that doesn't affect your mental or physical health.

If you are going to continue helping the person, it is important to set clear boundaries. Make sure that you are not compromising your own mental or physical health. Be firm about your boundaries and communicate them clearly.

Remember, you are not responsible for other people's lives. You have to take care of yourself first. It is okay to say no and it is okay to take care of your own needs.

If you still feel guilty after talking about your decision, ask yourself why you have stopped doing things for others. Is it because these things are not in your best interest, or are they causing you stress and anxiety? These are valid reasons to stop taking responsibility for things that aren't yours to take on. Once you have validated the reasons behind your decision, it will be easier to let go of the guilt.

Instead of dwelling on the negative feelings of guilt, try to focus on the positive aspects of your decision. Remind yourself of the benefits of prioritizing yourself and the positive changes that it can bring to your life.

It is important to be kind and compassionate to yourself, especially when you are going through challenging situations. You must acknowledge your feelings and accept them without judgment. Self-compassion involves being patient with yourself, accepting your faults, and treating yourself with the same kindness and understanding that we would offer to others.

By understanding the difference between healthy and unhealthy guilt, practicing self-compassion, setting boundaries, and focusing on the positive, we can navigate these feelings and prioritize our own well-being. Remember, taking care of ourselves is not a selfish act, but rather a necessary one.

A MEDITATION ON ELIMINATING FEELINGS OF GUILT

Take a few deep breaths, inhaling through your nose and exhaling through your mouth. As you do this, bring your attention to the sensation of the air moving in and out of your body. Notice how your chest rises and falls with each breath, and how your body begins to relax.

Now, bring your attention to your body. Scan your body from head to toe, noticing any areas of tension or discomfort.

As you exhale, release any tension you're holding in your body.

Allow your body to relax and become calm.

As you continue to breathe deeply and steadily, bring to mind a situation that is causing you to feel guilty.

It could be something you said or did or something you failed to do.

Notice any negative emotions that arise as you think about this situation.

Without judgment, allow those feelings to come and go.

Now, visualize yourself standing in front of a river. The water is clear and calm, and you can see the bottom of the river.

Imagine placing the situation that's causing you to feel guilty in a small wooden boat.

Place the boat gently onto the river and watch as it floats away from you, down the river.

As you watch the boat float away, imagine that you're releasing the guilt and negative emotions associated with it.

Allow yourself to feel lighter and more free as the boat disappears from view.

Now, bring to mind a positive memory or experience. It could be a time when you felt proud of yourself, accomplished a goal, or received recognition for your efforts.

Allow yourself to fully immerse in this memory, noticing how it makes you feel.

As you continue to breathe deeply, focus on the positive emotions associated with this memory.

Allow those feelings to expand and fill your body, replacing any feelings of guilt or negativity.

Forgive yourself.

Recognize that you are human and that you make mistakes.

Everyone does.

Allow yourself to feel compassion and understanding for yourself, and forgive yourself for whatever it is that is causing you to feel guilty.

Repeat to yourself:

"I forgive myself. I release this guilt. I am free."

Take a few more deep breaths, allowing yourself to fully

absorb the positive emotions and sensations in your body.

When you're ready, slowly open your eyes and return to the present moment.

THE IMPORTANCE OF SELF CARE

Taking on too much responsibility pushes us to the point of exhaustion, trying to be everything to everyone, and neglecting our own care.

It is essential to understand that self-care is not selfish, but rather it is a necessity for a healthy mind and body. Self-care is not just about taking a break or pampering yourself. It's about taking care of your physical, mental, and emotional health. Self-care is not a luxury, but a necessity.

When you neglect your own needs, you become more prone to stress, burnout, and health problems. Taking time for yourself allows you to recharge your batteries and show up as your best self in all areas of your life. When you take care of yourself, you are better able to care for others and fulfill your responsibilities.

When we take care of ourselves, we can time out for ourselves, indulge in activities that bring us joy, prioritize ourselves better, and maintain healthy relationships with others. Self-care can improve communication, reduce conflict, and enhance intimacy.

Self-care involves prioritizing one's overall well-being, which includes emotional and mental health, physical health, and social health. It involves taking time out for yourself, indulging in activities that bring you joy, and prioritizing yourself.

Self-care is essential for healing your body and mind, as it helps you deal with stress, anxiety, and other mental health issues that can negatively impact your overall health. When we take care of ourselves, we can better manage stress, improve our physical health, and improve our overall quality of life.

Self-care is any activity that we engage in to promote our physical, mental, and emotional well-being. This can include a wide range of practices, from getting enough sleep and exercise to practicing mindfulness, yoga, deep breathing, and relaxation techniques.

Self-care practices such as meditation, yoga, and deep breathing can help to reduce stress and promote a sense of calm and relaxation. We'll go into more depth with these self-care practices in future chapters.

Protecting your peace is an essential part of self-care for your mental and emotional well-being. We can experience stress, anxiety, and even depression when our peace is disturbed.

When we are dealing with stressful situations, it's challenging to maintain our peace. Chronic stress can lead to high blood pressure, heart disease, obesity, and depression.

Drama can be incredibly self-destructive. Drama can be in the form of gossip, rumors, or conflicts. When we are involved in drama, it can be stressful and can take up a lot of our time and energy. Distancing ourselves from people who bring drama into our lives is a form of self-care.

Avoiding negative people who always see the glass as half-empty can help reduce our stress levels. Negative people complain about everything and are always criticizing others. Being around negative people can be draining and can affect our mood. We can feel that we need to fix the things that the negative person is complaining about. This sets us back in a position of being responsible for things that aren't ours to bear.

Journaling, practicing gratitude, and engaging in hobbies can help to boost mental health. These practices can improve mood, reduce symptoms of depression and anxiety, and promote a sense of well-being.

I've included meditations in this book because mindfulness and meditation can help to reduce stress and promote a sense of calm and relaxation. These practices involve focusing on the present moment and cultivating a non-judgmental awareness of our thoughts and feelings. Meditating on a subject can also help us to make changes that stick.

Self-care is essential for maintaining good physical and mental health. By prioritizing self-care practices such as mindfulness, exercise, sleep, and healthy eating, you can improve your overall well-being and enhance your ability to manage stress, maintain healthy relationships, and perform at your best.

In the following chapters, we'll explore how yoga, deep breathing, EFT, and meditation can help you in your quest to stop taking responsibility for things that aren't your own and release guilt, stress, and stored trauma.

A Meditation on Protecting My Peace

Close your eyes and take a deep breath in through your nose, filling your lungs with air.

Hold your breath for a few seconds, and then exhale slowly through your mouth, releasing any tension or stress that you may be holding in your body.

Now, visualize a bright white light surrounding you. This light represents your inner peace, and it serves as a protective shield against any negative energy that may enter your space.

Take a moment to feel the warmth and comfort of this light.

As you continue to breathe deeply, repeat the following affirmations to yourself:

I am safe and protected.

I am calm and at peace.

I release all worries and fears.

I trust in the universe to guide me.

Visualize any negative thoughts or emotions leaving your body and being replaced by this sense of peace and protection.

Allow yourself to fully embrace this feeling, and know that you can return to it at any time.

Now, turn your attention to your physical body.

Scan your body from head to toe, and notice any areas of tension or discomfort.

As you exhale, release any tension you may be holding in your body.

Imagine each breath carrying away any stress or negativity.

As you continue to breathe deeply, visualize a protective bubble forming around you. This bubble is a shield that will protect you from any negative energy or distractions that may try to penetrate your mind and disrupt your peace.

Imagine this bubble expanding and growing stronger with each breath you take.

It is a beautiful, iridescent color that radiates light and positivity.

As you sit within this bubble, you feel safe, secure, and at peace.

Now, as you focus on your breathing, imagine any negative thoughts or emotions that may be weighing you down, floating away from you, and disappearing into the distance.

You are letting go of any worries or fears that may be obstructing your peace.

As you exhale, repeat the following affirmation to yourself: "I am protected, and my peace is secure."

Repeat this affirmation several times, allowing it to sink deep into your subconscious.

Now, take another deep breath in and feel the warmth and

light of the protective bubble surrounding you. As you exhale, release any remaining tension or stress, and allow yourself to sink deeper into a state of peace and relaxation.

Take a few more deep breaths, and when you are ready, slowly open your eyes.

Take a moment to appreciate the sense of calm and peace you have created within yourself.

YOGA TO RELEASE STRESSS AND TRAUMA IN OUR BODIES

Taking on too much responsibility that isn't yours can be overwhelming and can leave you feeling drained and stressed. This can often lead to physical symptoms such as headaches, muscle tension, chronic pain, and autoimmune issues. Additionally, constantly carrying the weight of others' responsibilities can lead to emotional trauma that can be difficult to overcome. This is where yoga comes in.

Yoga is a practice that can help you release stress and tension from your body and mind. The physical postures, or asanas, help to stretch and strengthen your muscles while also calming your nervous system. Through the practice of yoga, you can learn to connect with your breath and find a sense of calm amidst the chaos.

But yoga isn't just about the physical practice. The philosophy of yoga is deeply rooted in self-care and compassion. It encourages us to take time for ourselves and prioritize our own well-being. This is especially important for those who have taken on too much responsibility that isn't theirs. By prioritizing self-care, you can begin to heal from the emotional trauma that may have resulted from taking on too much or from being in a dysfunctional relationship.

Of course, it can be difficult to prioritize self-care when you feel like you have so many responsibilities to handle. This is where yoga can be especially helpful. By carving out just a few minutes each day for your yoga practice, you can begin to shift your mindset and prioritize yourself. You may find that as you begin to take care of yourself, you are better able to handle the responsibilities that you have taken on or find the strength to enforce the boundaries you have set.

In addition to the physical and emotional benefits of yoga, the practice also offers a sense of community. Many yoga studios and classes offer a supportive environment where you can connect with others who are also on a journey of self-care and healing. This sense of community can be incredibly healing and can help you feel less alone in your struggles.

Trauma can manifest itself in many ways, including feelings

of anxiety, depression, and even physical pain. By practicing yoga, we can learn to release these negative emotions and experiences from our bodies, allowing us to heal and move forward with our lives. Through breathing techniques, mindful movement, and meditation, we can learn to tune into our bodies and notice the physical sensations associated with stress and trauma. This awareness is the first step in releasing tension and promoting healing.

Breathing techniques, or pranayama, are an essential part of any yoga practice. Deep breathing signals our nervous system to relax, and it can be especially helpful for releasing tension in the muscles of the chest, neck, and shoulders. One simple technique is to inhale deeply through the nose, filling the lungs completely, and then exhale slowly through the mouth, releasing all the air. Repeat for several breaths, allowing the body to relax and release tension.

Yoga poses, or asanas, can be helpful for releasing stress and trauma. Certain poses, such as forward bends and hip openers, can release tension in the lower back and hips, where stress and trauma often manifest. Other poses, such as heart openers and back bends, can open up the chest and promote deep breathing.

It's important to approach these poses mindfully and with an awareness of your body's limits. It's not about achieving the perfect pose, but about listening to your body and finding what feels good.

There are many yoga poses that can help release stress and trauma stored in our bodies. Here are a few poses you can try:

Child's pose is a gentle stretch for the back, hips, and thighs. To do this pose, start on your hands and knees with your hands shoulder-width apart and your knees hip-width apart. Slowly lower your hips back towards your heels and stretch your arms out in front of you. Rest your forehead on the mat and take slow, deep breaths. Hold this pose for 30 seconds to one minute.

Standing forward fold is a great way to release tension in the neck, shoulders, and back. To do this pose, start in a standing position with your feet hip-width apart. Slowly fold forward from the hips and bring your hands to the ground or to your shins. Let your head hang heavy and take slow, deep breaths. Hold this pose for 30 seconds to one minute.

Downward-facing dog is a full-body stretch that can help to relieve tension in the back, shoulders, and neck. To do this pose, start on your hands and knees with your hands shoulder-width apart and your knees hip-width apart. Lift your hips up towards the ceiling and press your heels towards the ground. Keep your head between your arms and take slow, deep breaths. Hold this pose for 30 seconds to one minute.

Cat-cow pose is a gentle stretch for the spine and can help to release tension in the back and neck. To do this pose, start on your hands and knees with your hands shoulder-width apart and your knees hip-width apart. Inhale and arch your back, bringing your head up towards the ceiling. Exhale and round your spine, bringing your head towards your knees. Repeat this movement for 30 seconds to one minute.

Tree pose helps to improve balance and focus. It can also help to relieve stress and anxiety. To do this pose, start in a standing position with your feet hip-width apart. Lift one foot and place it on the inside of your opposite thigh. Bring your hands to your heart in prayer position and focus on a point in front of you. Take slow, deep breaths and hold this pose for 30 seconds to one minute. Repeat on the other side.

Bridge pose is a gentle back bend that can help to release tension in the back and neck. To do this pose, lie on your back with your knees bent and feet flat on the ground. Slowly lift your hips up towards the ceiling and interlace your hands under your back. Keep your shoulders on the ground and take slow, deep breaths. Hold this pose for 30 seconds to one minute.

Savasana is the final resting pose of a yoga practice, and it's a great way to release any remaining tension, fear, or trauma. To practice this posture, lie on your back with your arms and legs extended. Close your eyes and focus on your breath. Allow your body to relax completely and release any tension. Stay in the pose for at least five minutes, enjoying the sensation of peace and calm.

One area of the body that is particularly affected by stress and trauma is the psoas muscle. This muscle is located in the lower part of the spine, and it plays a critical role in our physical and emotional well-being. The psoas muscle handles several important functions in the body. It connects the spine to the pelvis and the legs, and it helps us to walk, run, and move our legs in different directions. It also supports the organs in our abdominal cavity and helps to regulate our breathing.

When we experience stress or trauma, our psoas muscles can

become tense and tight. This can lead to a range of physical and emotional symptoms, including back pain, hip pain, digestive problems, anxiety, and depression. By practicing yoga, we can learn to release tension in the psoas muscle and promote healing in our bodies and minds.

The psoas muscle is a deep muscle that runs from the lower back (lumbar spine) to the front of the hip joint. It's responsible for several important functions in the body, including:

Flexion of the hip joint: This action allows us to lift our legs and take steps.

Lateral rotation of the hip joint: This action allows us to turn our legs outward.

Stabilization of the lumbar spine: The psoas muscle helps to support the lower back and maintain good posture.

The psoas muscle is connected to the sympathetic nervous system, which is responsible for our "fight or flight" response. When we experience stress or trauma, our sympathetic nervous system is activated, and our psoas muscle contracts. This can lead to tightness and tension in the muscle, which can cause pain and discomfort.

There are several yoga poses that can help to release tension in the psoas muscle and promote healing. Here are five poses to try:

Low Lunge - Start in a high plank position, then step your right foot forward between your hands. Lower your left knee to the ground, and place your hands on your right knee. Sink your hips down towards the ground and feel the stretch in your left hip flexor (psoas muscle).

Warrior II - Stand with your feet hip-width apart, then step your left foot back about 3-4 feet. Turn your left foot out 90 degrees and bend your right knee so that it's directly over your ankle. Reach your arms out to the sides and gaze over your right hand. This pose stretches the hip flexors and strengthens the legs.

Bridge Pose - Lie on your back with your knees bent and your feet flat on the ground. Press your feet down into the ground, and lift your hips up towards the ceiling. Clasp your hands together underneath your back, and breathe deeply. This pose stretches the front of the hips and opens the chest.

Pigeon Pose - Start in a downward-facing dog position, then bring your right knee forward and place it behind your right wrist. Extend your left leg behind you, and lower your hips down towards the ground. This pose stretches the outer hip and glutes, as well as the psoas muscle.

Child's Pose - Start on your hands and knees, then lower your hips back towards your heels. Extend your arms forward and rest your forehead on the ground. Breathe deeply and relax. This pose releases tension in the lower back and hips, as well as the psoas muscle.

The psoas muscle is an important muscle that affects our bodies and minds in many ways. When we experience stress or trauma, our psoas muscles can become tight and painful, leading to discomfort and tension. Practicing yoga can be an effective way to release stress and trauma from our bodies, and there are specific yoga poses that can help to release tension in the psoas muscle. By incorporating these poses into your yoga practice, you can promote healing and release tension in your body and mind.

By combining breath work, movement, and mindfulness, a yoga practice can help you find greater peace and balance in your life.

If you're looking for a yoga practice to let go of tension, fear, and trauma, here's a sequence you can try:

Close your eyes and take a few deep breaths, inhaling through your nose and exhaling through your mouth. As you breathe, imagine yourself letting go of any tension or stress you may be holding onto.

The first pose in this sequence is the Standing Fold. This pose is a gentle way to stretch the hamstrings, calves, and lower back, which can become tense from sitting for extended periods of time or from stress.

Next, move into Downward Dog. This pose is an excellent way to stretch the entire body, from the hamstrings and calves to the shoulders and upper back.

After Downward Dog, move into Cat-Cow Pose. This pose is a great way to release tension in the spine and improve circulation

Next up is Tree Pose. This pose is an excellent way to improve balance and focus, as well as release tension in the hips and legs.

After Tree Pose, move into Low Lunge.

This pose is an excellent way to stretch the hip flexors and release tension in the hips and legs.

To perform Low Lunge, step one foot forward and bend your knee, keeping your back leg straight. Place your hands on the ground or on your knee, and hold for a few breaths, then switch sides.

Next up is Warrior II. This pose is an excellent way to strengthen the legs and improve stability, as well as release tension in the hips and shoulders.

After Warrior II, move into Pigeon's Pose. This pose is an

excellent way to release tension in the hips and improve flexibility. After completing one side, extend your other leg behind you and hold for a few breaths, then switch sides.

From Pigeon's Post move into Bridge Pose. Bridge Pose is an excellent way to release tension in the lower back and improve circulation.

After Bridge Pose, move into Child's Pose. This pose is an excellent way to release tension in the neck, shoulders, and back, as well as promote relaxation.

Finally, end your practice with Savasana.

This pose is an essential part of any yoga practice, as it allows you to fully relax and let go of any remaining tension or stress.

Remember to focus on your breath throughout the practice and allow it to guide your movements. With consistent practice, you may find that you are able to release tension and trauma more easily and find a greater sense of peace and balance in your life.

For those who have experienced trauma, yoga can be a safe and gentle way to begin the healing process. Trauma-sensitive yoga takes into account the unique needs of those who have experienced trauma and focuses on creating a safe and supportive environment. Classes may be smaller and more intimate, and teachers may offer modifications or options for poses that may be triggering.

If you're interested in trying yoga for stress or trauma, look for classes that are labeled as "gentle" "trauma-informed" or "restorative." These classes will be slower-paced and more focused on relaxation than on physical exertion. And remember, yoga is not about achieving the perfect pose or being the most flexible person in the room. It's about tuning into your body and finding what feels good for you.

DEEP BREATHING EXERCISES

Deep breathing exercises have been proven to be an effective way to manage stress and anxiety. When we breathe deeply, we activate the parasympathetic nervous system which promotes relaxation and calmness. When we feel overwhelmed, our breathing becomes shallow and quick. This can cause our bodies to go into a fight or flight response, making us feel even more stressed and anxious. However, by taking the time to do deep breathing exercises, we can slow down our breathing and calm our bodies, which can help us release the stress and trauma we are holding onto. Deep breathing helps to reduce the production of stress hormones such as cortisol and adrenaline which can have negative effects on our mental and physical health.

One of the main benefits of deep breathing exercises is that they help us focus on the present moment. When we are overwhelmed with responsibilities, we may find ourselves constantly worrying about the future or dwelling on the past. However, by taking deep breaths and focusing on our breath, we can bring ourselves back to the present moment and let go of those worries.

If you are struggling with setting or enforcing boundaries, practicing deep breathing can help you to relax and stay in control of your emotions while having uncomfortable discussions.

Deep breathing exercises help to increase oxygen levels in the body, which can improve mental clarity, reduce anxiety, and promote feelings of calmness and can help to improve mindfulness and focus, which can help you to better manage stress and trauma.

Here are some deep breathing techniques that can help you to relax, release stress, and help you stay calm in stressful situations:

Diaphragmatic breathing, also known as Belly Breathing, is a simple technique that involves breathing deeply through the nose, filling the lungs, and expanding the belly. To perform this exercise, sit or lie down in a comfortable position. Place one hand on your belly and the other on your chest. Inhale slowly through your nose, filling your lungs with air and allowing your belly to expand. Hold your breath for a few seconds and then exhale slowly through your mouth, allowing your belly to deflate. Repeat this exercise for five to ten minutes. This technique can help reduce tension in your upper body and promote feelings of relaxation.

Counting breaths is another simple technique that involves counting your breaths as you inhale and exhale. To perform this exercise, sit or lie down in a comfortable position. Inhale deeply through your nose, counting to four. Hold your breath for a few seconds and then exhale slowly through your mouth, counting to six. Repeat this exercise for five to ten minutes.

Square Breathing, also known as Box Breathing, is a technique that involves inhaling, holding, exhaling, and holding for equal counts. To perform this exercise, sit or lie down in a comfortable position. Inhale slowly through your nose, counting to four. Hold your breath for a count of four. Exhale slowly through your mouth, counting to four. Hold your breath for a count of four. Repeat this exercise for five to ten minutes. This technique can help slow down your heart rate and promote a sense of calm.

Alternate nostril breathing is a technique that involves closing one nostril with your thumb and inhaling deeply through the other nostril. Then, close that nostril with your ring finger and exhale through the other nostril. Repeat this cycle for a few minutes to balance your nervous system and reduce stress.

4-7-8 breathing is a technique that involves inhaling deeply through your nose for four seconds, holding your breath for seven seconds, and exhaling slowly through your mouth for eight seconds. Repeat this cycle for a few minutes to calm your mind and body.

Deep breathing exercises are a simple yet effective way to release stress and trauma from the body that can be done anywhere. By activating the parasympathetic nervous system, increasing oxygen levels, and improving mindfulness, deep breathing exercises can help you to better manage stress and trauma in you daily lives.

EFT, EMOTIONAL FREEDOM TECHNIQUE

The Emotional Freedom Technique (EFT) is an effective tool to reduce your levels of stress and anxiety. EFT, also known as tapping, is a form of psychological acupressure that involves tapping or massaging specific points on your body, while focusing on the emotional distress or negative feelings you are experiencing. EFT combines elements of traditional Chinese medicine, cognitive therapy, and acupressure and works by tapping into the body's energy system.

The goal of EFT is to release negative emotions and beliefs that are causing stress and tension in the body.

According to traditional Chinese medicine, the body has a network of energy channels called meridians. These meridians are connected to different organs and systems in the body. When energy is flowing freely through these channels, we feel healthy and balanced. But when the flow of energy is blocked or disrupted, we experience physical and emotional symptoms. By tapping on specific acupressure points on the body, EFT helps to release these blockages and restore the flow of energy. This can help to ease stress, anxiety, and other negative emotions.

EFT is an effective tool for managing stress and anxiety. Research has found that EFT can reduce cortisol levels (the hormone associated with stress) and improve overall well-being.

In one study, participants who used EFT for just one hour had a significant decrease in cortisol (the stress hormone) levels compared to a control group. Dawson Church, Ph.D., conducted this study with 83 participants divided into two groups. One group received an hour-long EFT session, while the other group watched a relaxing video. The results showed the EFT group had a significant decrease in cortisol levels compared to the control group.

Another study found that EFT was effective in reducing PTSD symptoms in veterans. After just 6 EFT sessions, participants reported a significant decrease in symptoms, such as nightmares, flashbacks, and hyper-vigilance. Church conducted a study that focused on 59 veterans suffering from PTSD. They divided the participants into two groups, one received EFT therapy, while the other received standard care. The results showed the EFT group had a significant decrease in PTSD symptoms compared to the control group.

You can use EFT for a wide range of issues, including stress management, anxiety, depression, PTSD, phobias, addiction, and chronic pain. It can also address limiting beliefs and negative self-talk that may hold you back.

It is a non-invasive and drug-free therapy that people can learn easily and practice at home. One of the key benefits of EFT is that it is a self-administered technique that can be done anytime, anywhere. This makes it a convenient and accessible tool. You don't need any special equipment or training to do it.

Traumatic events that have not been processed can appear as physical tightness, psychological distress, or persistent pain in the body. This can lead to a range of symptoms, including anxiety, depression, and chronic pain. By tapping on specific points on the body while focusing on the traumatic experience, EFT can help to release the physical and emotional tension associated with trauma. This can help to reduce symptoms and improve overall well-being.

If you're interested in trying EFT, here's a simple process to follow:

Identify the issue - Start by identifying the issue or problem you want to work on. This could be a specific stressor or a traumatic experience.

Rate the intensity - On a scale of 0-10, rate the intensity of the issue. This will help you track progress as you work through the EFT process.

Create a setup statement - Create a statement that acknowledges the problem and affirms your self-acceptance. For example, "Even though I feel anxious about this situation, I deeply and completely accept myself."

Tap on the points - Using your fingertips, tap on the acupressure points. You tap each point about 7 times while focusing on the issue.

The tapping points are:

After tapping on all points, you take a deep breath and rate the intensity of the issue again. If it's still high, you can repeat the process until you feel a shift in your emotions or physical sensations.

As you tap, repeat a statement or affirmation related to the issue. For example, "Even though I feel stressed and overwhelmed, I deeply and completely accept myself."

Re-rate the intensity - After tapping on the points for a few rounds, re-rate the intensity of the issue. If it's still high, continue tapping until the intensity drops to 0-2.

Repeat as needed - Depending on the issue, you may need to repeat the process multiple times to see lasting results.

Here are some example EFT statements that can help you release this sense of responsibility:

1. Even though I feel responsible for everything, I deeply and completely love and accept myself.

2. Even though I feel like I need to be in control of everything, I choose to release this need and trust that everything will work out.

3. Even though I feel like I need to take care of everyone, I choose to prioritize my own needs and trust that others are capable of taking care of themselves.

4. Even though I feel like I need to fix everything, I choose to release this pressure and trust that everything will work out in the end.

5. Even though I feel like everything is my fault, I choose to release this burden and trust that things will work out.

Resentment towards others can be a particularly challenging emotion to deal with. It can eat away at us and cause us to hold grudges that can last a lifetime.

Here are some example EFT statements that can help you release resentment:

1. Even though I feel resentful towards [person's name], I choose to forgive them and release this resentment. I deeply and completely love and accept myself.

2. Even though I feel like [person's name] has wronged me, I choose to release this anger and move on with my life.

3. Even though I feel like [person's name] owes me something, I choose to release this expectation and focus on my own happiness.

4. Even though I feel like [person's name] has caused me pain, I choose to release this pain and focus on healing myself.

5. Even though I feel angry and bitter about what happened, I choose to release this resentment and find peace within myself.

6. Even though I feel angry and bitter about what happened, I choose to release this resentment and find peace within myself.

7. Even though I feel justified in my anger, I choose to let go of this negative emotion.

Guilt is another emotion that can be incredibly difficult to deal with. It can stem from a variety of sources, including our own actions, the actions of others, and societal expectations.

Here are some example EFT statements that can help you release guilt:

1. Even though I feel guilty about [situation], I choose to forgive myself and release this guilt. I deeply and completely love and accept myself.

2. Even though I feel like I should have done things differently, I choose to accept that I did the best I could with what I

had.

3. Even though I feel like I've done something wrong, I choose to release this guilt and learn from my mistakes.

4. Even though I feel like I've let [person's name] down, I choose to release this guilt and focus on moving forward.

5. Even though I feel guilty for taking care of myself, I choose to prioritize my own needs and trust that this is the best thing for me.

6. Even though I feel like I don't deserve forgiveness, I choose to forgive myself and move forward with love and compassion.

You can use these example EFT statements as a road map toward making statements that resonate with you and the issues that you are working on.

EFT is a powerful tool for managing stress and releasing trauma from the body. If you're interested in trying EFT, there are many resources available online and in person. It's important to find a qualified EFT practitioner who can guide you through the process and ensure that you're using the technique safely.

RESOURCES

If you're feeling overwhelmed or like you can't set boundaries on your own, seek support. Talk to a friend, family member, or therapist who can help you navigate the process. Remember, you don't have to do everything on your own.

If you do not feel safe speaking up and setting limits and boundaries in your relationship, seek outside support. It's important to remember that domestic violence is never okay and that there are resources available to help you.

If you are in an abusive relationship, seek help immediately.

Here are some resources that can help:

If you're in immediate danger, call 911.

If you are in crisis, call:
National Domestic Violence Hotline: 1-800-799-SAFE (7233) This hotline provides crisis intervention, safety planning, and referrals to local resources.

Other resources are:

RAINN (Rape, Abuse & Incest National Network): 1-800-656-HOPE (4673)

The National Coalition Against Domestic Violence: (303) 839-1852

You can also reach out to a local shelter or hotline for support and guidance.

Made in the USA
Columbia, SC
22 April 2024